On
Business
Model
Innovation

HBR's 10 Must Reads series is the definitive collection of ideas and best practices for aspiring and experienced leaders alike. These books offer essential reading selected from the pages of *Harvard Business Review* on topics critical to the success of every manager.

Titles include:

HBR's 10 Must Reads 2015
HBR's 10 Must Reads 2016
HBR's 10 Must Reads 2017
HBR's 10 Must Reads 2018
HBR's 10 Must Reads 2019
HBR's 10 Must Reads 2020
HBR's 10 Must Reads for CEOs
HBR's 10 Must Reads for New Managers
HBR's 10 Must Reads on AI, Analytics, and the New Machine Age
HBR's 10 Must Reads on Business Model Innovation
HBR's 10 Must Reads on Change Management
HBR's 10 Must Reads on Collaboration
HBR's 10 Must Reads on Communication
HBR's 10 Must Reads on Diversity
HBR's 10 Must Reads on Emotional Intelligence
HBR's 10 Must Reads on Entrepreneurship and Startups
HBR's 10 Must Reads on Innovation
HBR's 10 Must Reads on Leadership
HBR's 10 Must Reads on Leadership for Healthcare
HBR's 10 Must Reads on Leadership Lessons from Sports
HBR's 10 Must Reads on Making Smart Decisions
HBR's 10 Must Reads on Managing Across Cultures
HBR's 10 Must Reads on Managing People
HBR's 10 Must Reads on Managing Yourself
HBR's 10 Must Reads on Mental Toughness
HBR's 10 Must Reads on Negotiation
HBR's 10 Must Reads on Nonprofits and the Social Sectors

On
Business
Model
Innovation

HARVARD BUSINESS REVIEW PRESS
Boston, Massachusetts

HBR Press Quantity Sales Discounts

Harvard Business Review Press titles are available at significant quantity discounts when purchased in bulk for client gifts, sales promotions, and premiums. Special editions, including books with corporate logos, customized covers, and letters from the company or CEO printed in the front matter, as well as excerpts of existing books, can also be created in large quantities for special needs.

For details and discount information for both print and ebook formats, contact booksales@harvardbusiness.org, tel. 800-988-0886, or www.hbr.org/bulksales.

The web addresses referenced in this book were live and correct at the time of the book's publication but may be subject to change.

Library of Congress Cataloging-in-Publication Data is forthcoming

ISBN: 978-1-63369-687-7
eISBN: 978-1-63369-688-4

The paper used in this publication meets the requirements of the American National Standard for Permanence of Paper for Publications and Documents in Libraries and Archives Z39.48-1992.

Contents

On
**Business
Model
Innovation**

Why Business Models Matter

by Joan Magretta

"BUSINESS MODEL" was one of the great buzzwords of the Internet boom, routinely invoked, as the writer Michael Lewis put it, "to glorify all manner of half-baked plans." A company didn't need a strategy, or a special competence, or even any customers—all it needed was a Web-based business model that promised wild profits in some distant, ill-defined future. Many people—investors, entrepreneurs, and executives alike—bought the fantasy and got burned. And as the inevitable counterreaction played out, the concept of the business model fell out of fashion nearly as quickly as the .com appendage itself.

That's a shame. For while it's true that a lot of capital was raised to fund flawed business models, the fault lies not with the concept of the business model but with its distortion and misuse. A good business model remains essential to every successful organization, whether it's a new venture or an established player. But before managers can apply the concept, they need a simple working definition that clears up the fuzziness associated with the term.

Telling a Good Story

The word "model" conjures up images of white boards covered with arcane mathematical formulas. Business models, though, are anything but arcane. They are, at heart, stories—stories that explain how enterprises work. A good business model answers Peter Drucker's age-old questions: Who is the customer? And what does the customer value? It also answers the fundamental questions every manager must ask: How do we make money in this business? What is the underlying economic logic that explains how we can deliver value to customers at an appropriate cost?

Consider the story behind one of the most successful business models of all time: that of the traveler's check. During a European vacation in 1892, J.C. Fargo, the president of American Express, had a hard time translating his letters of credit into cash. "The moment I got off the beaten path," he said on his return, "they were no more use than so much wet wrapping paper. If the president of American Express has that sort of trouble, just think what ordinary travelers face. Something has got to be done about it."[1] What American Express did was to create the traveler's check—and from that innovation evolved a robust business model with all the elements of a good story: precisely delineated characters, plausible motivations, and a plot that turns on an insight about value.

The story was straightforward for customers. In exchange for a small fee, travelers could buy both peace of mind (the checks were insured against loss and theft) and convenience (they were very widely accepted). Merchants also played a key role in the tale. They accepted the checks because they trusted the American Express name, which was like a universal letter of credit, and because, by accepting them, they attracted more customers. The more other merchants accepted the checks, the stronger any individual merchant's motivation became not to be left out.

As for American Express, it had discovered a riskless business, because customers always paid cash for the checks. Therein lies the twist to the plot, the underlying economic logic that turned what would have been an unremarkable operation into a money machine. The twist was *float*. In most businesses, costs precede revenues: Before anyone can buy your product, you've got to build it and pay for it. The traveler's check turned the normal cycle of debt and risk on its head. Because people paid for the checks before (often long before) they used them, American Express was getting

WHY BUSINESS MODELS MATTER

Idea in Brief

"Business model" was one of the great buzzwords of the Internet boom. A company didn't need a strategy, a special competence, or even any customers—all it needed was a Web-based business model that promised wild profits in some distant, ill-defined future. Many people—investors, entrepreneurs, and executives alike—got burned. And as the inevitable counter-reaction played out, the concept of the business model quickly fell out of fashion.

That's a shame, because a good business model remains essential to every successful organization, whether it's a new venture or an established player. Business models are, at heart, stories that explain

how enterprises work. Like a good story, a robust business model contains precisely delineated characters, plausible motivations, and a plot that turns on an insight about value. It answers certain questions: Who is the customer? How do we make money? What underlying economic logic explains how we can deliver value to customers at an appropriate cost?

A business model isn't a strategy, even though many people use the terms interchangeably. Business models describe, as a system, how the pieces of a business fit together. But they don't factor in one critical dimension of performance: competition. That's the job of strategy.

something banks had long enjoyed—the equivalent of an interest-free loan from its customers. Moreover, some of the checks were never cashed, giving the company an extra windfall.

As this story shows, a successful business model represents a better way than the existing alternatives. It may offer more value to a discrete group of customers. Or it may completely replace the old way of doing things and become the standard for the next generation of entrepreneurs to beat. Nobody today would head off on vacation armed with a suitcase full of letters of credit. Fargo's business model changed the rules of the game, in this case, the economics of travel. By eliminating the fear of being robbed and the hours spent trying to get cash in a strange city, the checks removed a significant barrier to travel, helping many more people to take many more trips. Like all really powerful business models, this one didn't just shift existing revenues among companies; it created new, incremental demand. Traveler's checks remained the preferred method for taking money abroad for decades, until a new technology—the automated teller machine—granted travelers even greater convenience.

Creating a business model is, then, a lot like writing a new story. At some level, all new stories are variations on old ones, reworkings of the universal themes underlying all human experience. Similarly, all new business models are variations on the generic value chain underlying all businesses. Broadly speaking, this chain has two parts. Part one includes all the activities associated with making something: designing it, purchasing raw materials, manufacturing, and so on. Part two includes all the activities associated with selling something: finding and reaching customers, transacting a sale, distributing the product or delivering the service. A new business model's plot may turn on designing a new product for an unmet need, as it did with the traveler's check. Or it may turn on a process innovation, a better way of making or selling or distributing an already proven product or service.

Think about the simple business that direct-marketing pioneer Michael Bronner created in 1980 when he was a junior at Boston University. Like his classmates, Bronner had occasionally bought books of discount coupons for local stores and restaurants. Students paid a small fee for the coupon books. But Bronner had a better idea. Yes, the books created value for students, but they had the potential to create much more value for merchants, who stood to gain by increasing their sales of pizza and haircuts. Bronner realized that the key to unlocking that potential was wider distribution—putting a coupon book in every student's backpack.

That posed two problems. First, as Bronner well knew, students were often strapped for cash. Giving the books away for free would solve that problem. Second, Bronner needed to get the books to students at a cost that wouldn't eat up his profits. So he made a clever proposal to the dean of Boston University's housing department: Bronner would assemble the coupon books and deliver them in bulk to the housing department, and the department could distribute them free to every dorm on campus. This would make the department look good in the eyes of the students, a notoriously tough crowd to please. The dean agreed.

Now Bronner could make an even more interesting proposal to neighborhood business owners. If they agreed to pay a small fee to appear in the new book, their coupons would be seen by all 14,000 residents of BU's dorms. Bronner's idea took off. Before long, he had extended the concept to other campuses, then to downtown office buildings. Eastern Exclusives, his first company, was born. His innovation wasn't the coupon book but his business model; it worked because he had insight into the motivations of three sets of characters: students, merchants, and school administrators.

Tying Narrative to Numbers

The term "business model" first came into widespread use with the advent of the personal computer and the spreadsheet. Before the spreadsheet, business planning usually meant producing a single, base-case forecast. At best, you did a little sensitivity analysis around the projection. The spreadsheet ushered in a much more analytic approach to planning because every major line item could be pulled apart, its components and subcomponents analyzed and tested. You could ask what-if questions about the critical assumptions on which your business depended—for example, what if customers are more price-sensitive than we thought?—and with a few keystrokes, you could see how any change would play out on every aspect of the whole. In other words, you could model the behavior of a business.

This was something new. Before the personal computer changed the nature of business planning, most successful business models, like Fargo's, were created more by accident than by design and forethought. The business model became clear only after the fact. By enabling companies to tie their marketplace insights much more tightly to the resulting economics—to link their assumptions about how people would behave to the numbers of a pro forma P&L— spreadsheets made it possible to model businesses *before* they were launched.

Of course, a spreadsheet is only as good as the assumptions that go into it. Once an enterprise starts operating, the underlying assumptions of its model—about both motivations and economics—are subjected to continuous testing in the marketplace. And success often hinges on management's ability to tweak, or even overhaul, the model on the fly. When EuroDisney opened its Paris theme park in 1992, it borrowed the business model that had worked so well in Disney's U.S. parks. Europeans, the company thought, would spend roughly the same amount of time and money per visit as Americans did on food, rides, and souvenirs.

Each of Disney's assumptions about the revenue side of the business turned out to be wrong. Europeans did not, for example, graze all day long at the park's various restaurants the way Americans did. Instead, they all expected to be seated at precisely the same lunch or dinner hour, which overloaded the facilities and created long lines of frustrated patrons. Because of those miscalculations, EuroDisney was something of a disaster in its early years. It became a success only after a dozen or so of the key elements in its business model were changed, one by one.

When managers operate consciously from a model of how the entire business system will work, every decision, initiative, and measurement provides valuable feedback. Profits are important not only for their own sake but also because they tell you whether your model is working. If you fail to achieve the results you expected, you reexamine your model, as EuroDisney did. Business modeling is, in this sense, the managerial equivalent of the scientific method—you start with a hypothesis, which you then test in action and revise when necessary.

Two Critical Tests

When business models don't work, it's because they fail either the narrative test (the story doesn't make sense) or the numbers test (the P&L doesn't add up). The business model of on-line grocers, for instance, failed the numbers test. The grocery industry has very thin margins to begin with, and on-line merchants like Webvan incurred new costs for marketing, service, delivery, and technology. Since customers weren't willing to pay significantly more for groceries bought on-line than in stores, there was no way the math could work. Internet grocers had plenty of company. Many ventures in the first wave of electronic commerce failed simply because the basic business math was flawed.

Other business models failed the narrative test. Consider the rapid rise and fall of Priceline Webhouse Club. This was an offshoot of Priceline.com, the company that introduced name-your-own pricing to the purchase of airline tickets. Wall Street's early enthusiasm encouraged CEO Jay Walker to extend his concept to groceries and gasoline.

Here's the story Walker tried to tell. Via the Web, millions of consumers would tell him how much they wanted to pay for, say, a jar of peanut butter. Consumers could specify the price but not the brand, so they might end up with Jif or they might end up with Skippy. Webhouse would then aggregate the bids and go to companies like P&G and Bestfoods and try to make a deal: Take 50 cents off the price of your peanut butter, and we'll order a million jars this week. Webhouse wanted to be a power broker for individual consumers: Representing millions of shoppers, it would negotiate discounts and then pass on the savings to its customers, taking a fee in the process.

What was wrong with the story? It assumed that companies like P&G, Kimberly-Clark, and Exxon wanted to play this game. Think about that for a minute. Big consumer companies have spent decades and billions of dollars building brand loyalty. The Webhouse model teaches consumers to buy on price alone. So why would the manufacturers want to help Webhouse undermine both their prices and the brand identities they'd worked so hard to build? They wouldn't. The story just didn't make sense. To be a power broker, Webhouse needed a huge base of loyal customers. To get those customers, it first needed to deliver discounts. Since the consumer product companies refused to play, Webhouse had to pay for those discounts out of its own pocket. A few hundred million dollars later, in October 2000, it ran out of cash—and out of investors who still believed the story.

In case anyone thinks that Internet entrepreneurs have a monopoly on flawed business models, think again. We tend to forget about ideas that don't pan out, but business history is littered with them. In the 1980s, the one-stop financial supermarket was a business model that fired the imagination of many executives—but Sears, to cite one example, discovered that its customers just didn't get the connection between power tools and annuities. In the 1990s, Silicon Graphics invested hundreds of millions of dollars in interactive television, but it was unable to find real customers who were as enchanted by the technology as the engineers who invented it. Ultimately, models like these fail because they are built on faulty assumptions about customer behavior. They are solutions in search of a problem.

The irony about the slipshod use of the concept of business models is that when used correctly, it actually forces managers to think rigorously about their businesses. A business model's great strength as a planning tool is that it focuses attention on how all the elements of the system fit into a working whole. It's no surprise that, even during the Internet boom, executives who grasped the basics of business model thinking were in a better position to lead the winners. Meg Whitman, for example, joined eBay in its early days because she was struck by what she described as "the emotional connection between eBay users and the site."[2] The way people behaved was an early indicator of the potential power of the eBay brand. Whitman also realized that eBay, unlike many Internet businesses that were being created, simply "couldn't be done off-line." In other words, Whitman—a seasoned executive—saw a compelling, coherent narrative with the potential to be translated into a profitable business.

Whitman has remained attentive to the psychology and the economics that draw collectors, bargain hunters, community seekers, and small-business people to eBay. Its auction model succeeds not just because the Internet lowers the cost of connecting vast numbers of buyers and sellers but also because eBay has made decisions about the scope of its activities that result in an appropriate cost structure. After an auction, eBay leaves it to the sellers and buyers to work out the logistics of payment and shipping. The company never takes possession of the goods or carries any inventory. It incurs no transportation costs. It bears no credit risk. And it has none of the overhead that would come with those activities.

What About Strategy?

Every viable organization is built on a sound business model, whether or not its founders or its managers conceive of what they do in those terms. But a business model isn't the same thing as a strategy, even though many people use the terms interchangeably today. Business models describe, as a system, how the pieces of a business fit together. But they don't factor in one critical dimension of performance: competition. Sooner or later—and it is usually sooner—every enterprise runs into competitors. Dealing with that reality is strategy's job.

A competitive strategy explains how you will do better than your rivals. And doing better, by definition, means being different. Organizations achieve superior performance when they are unique, when they do something no other business does in ways that no other business can duplicate. When you cut away the jargon, that's what strategy is all about—how you are going to do better by being different. The logic is straightforward: When all companies offer the same products and services to the same customers by performing the same kinds of activities, no company will prosper. Customers will benefit, at least in the short term, while head-to-head competition drives prices down to a point where returns are inadequate. It was precisely this kind of competition—destructive competition, to use Michael Porter's term— that did in many Internet retailers, whether they were selling pet supplies, drugs, or toys. Too many fledgling companies rushed to market with identical business models and no strategies to differentiate themselves in terms of which customers and markets to serve, what products and services to offer, and what kinds of value to create.

To see the distinction between a strategy and a business model, you need only look at Wal-Mart. You might think that the giant retailer's success was a result of pioneering a new business model, but that's not the case. When Sam Walton opened his first Wal-Mart in 1962 in the hamlet of Rogers, Arkansas, the discount-retailing business model had been around for a few years. It had emerged in the mid-1950s, when a slew of industry pioneers (now long forgotten) began to apply supermarket logic to the sale of general merchandise.

Supermarkets had been educating customers since the 1930s about the value of giving up personal service in exchange for lower food prices, and the new breed of retailers saw that they could adapt the basic story line of the supermarket to clothing, appliances, and a host of other consumer goods. The idea was to offer lower prices than conventional department stores by slashing costs. And so the basic business model for discount retailing took shape: First, strip away the department store's physical amenities such as the carpeting and the chandeliers. Second, configure the stores to handle large numbers of shoppers efficiently. And third, put fewer salespeople on the floor and rely on customers to serve themselves. Do those things well, and you could offer low prices and still make money.

Walton heard about the new discount stores, visited a few, and liked their potential. In 1962, he decided to set out on his own, borrowing a lot of ideas for his early stores from Kmart and others. But it was what he chose to do differently—the ways he put his own stamp on the basic business model—that made Wal-Mart so fabulously successful. His model was the same as Kmart's, but his strategy was unique.

From the very start, for instance, Walton chose to serve a different group of customers in a different set of markets. The ten largest discounters in 1962, all gone today, focused on large metropolitan areas and cities like New York. Wal-Mart's "key strategy," in Walton's own words, "was to put good-sized stores into little one-horse towns which everybody else was ignoring."[3] He sought out isolated rural towns, like Rogers, with populations between 5,000 and 25,000. Being a small-town guy himself, Walton knew the terrain well. The nearest city was probably a four-hour drive away. He rightly bet that if his stores could match or beat the city prices, "people would shop at home." And since Wal-Mart's markets tended to be too small to support more than one large retailer, Walton was able to preempt competitors and discourage them from entering Wal-Mart's territory.

Wal-Mart also took a different approach to merchandising and pricing than its competitors did—that is, it promised customers a different kind of value. While competitors relied heavily on private label goods, second-tier brands, and price promotions, Wal-Mart promised national brands at everyday low prices. To make this promise more than a marketing slogan, the company pursued efficiency and reduced costs through innovative practices in areas such as purchasing, logistics, and information management.

The business model of discount retailing has attracted many players since it emerged in the 1950s. Most of them have failed. A few, like Wal-Mart and Target, have achieved superior performance over the long haul because their strategies set them apart. Wal-Mart offers branded goods for less to a carefully chosen customer base. Target built a strategy around a different kind of value—style and fashion. The losers in the industry—the chronic underperformers like Kmart—are companies that tried to be all things to all people. They failed to find distinctive ways to compete.

A Good Model Is Not Enough

There's another, more recent story that sheds further light on the relationship between business models and strategies. It's the story of Dell Computer. Unlike Sam Walton, Michael Dell was a true business-model pioneer. The model he created is, by now, well known: While other personal-computer makers sold through resellers, Dell sold directly to end customers. That not only cut out a costly link from the value chain, it also gave Dell the information it needed to manage inventory better than any other company in its industry. And because the pace of innovation in the industry was intense, Dell's inventory advantage meant it could avoid the high cost of obsolescence that other computer makers had to bear. Armed with its innovative business model, Dell has consistently outperformed rivals for more than a decade.

In this case, Dell's business model functioned much like a strategy: It made Dell different in ways that were hard to copy. If Dell's rivals tried to sell direct, they would disrupt their existing distribution channels and alienate the resellers on whom they relied. Trapped by their own strategies, they were damned if they copied Dell and damned if they didn't. When a new model changes the economics of an industry and is difficult to replicate, it can by itself create a strong competitive advantage.

What often gets lost in Dell's story, though, is the role that pure strategy has played in the company's superior performance. While Dell's direct business model laid out which value chain activities Dell would do (and which it wouldn't do), the company still had crucial strategic choices to make about which customers to serve and what kinds of products and services to offer. In the 1990s, for example, while other PC makers focused on computers for the home market, Dell consciously chose to go after large corporate accounts, which were far more profitable. Other PC makers offered low-end machines to lure in first-time buyers. Michael Dell wasn't interested in this "no-margin" business. He staked out his territory selling more powerful, higher margin computers.

Then, because Dell sold direct and could analyze its customers in depth, it began to notice that its average selling price to consumers was increasing while the industry's was falling. Consumers who were buying their second or third machines and who were looking for more power and less hand-holding were coming to Dell—even though it wasn't targeting them. Only in 1997, *after* it had a profitable, billion-dollar consumer business, did Dell dedicate a group to serving the consumer segment.

Now that everyone in its industry is selling direct, Dell's strategy has shifted to deal with the new competitive realities. With a decade-long lead, Dell is by far the industry's best executor of the direct-selling model—it is the low-cost producer. So it is using its cost advantage in PCs to compete on price, to gain share, and to drive the weaker players out of the business. At the same time, the company is relying on its core business model to pursue opportunities in new product markets, like servers, that have greater profit potential than PCs. The underlying business model remains the same. The strategic choices about where to apply the model—which geographic markets, which segments, which customers, which products—are what change.

Clarity about its business model has helped Dell in another way: as a basis for employee communication and motivation. Because a business model tells a good story, it can be used to get everyone in the organization aligned around the kind of value the company wants to create. Stories are easy to grasp and easy to remember. They help individuals to see their own jobs within the larger context of what the company is trying to do and to tailor their behavior accordingly. Used in this way, a good business model can become a powerful tool for improving execution.

———————

Today, "business model" and "strategy" are among the most sloppily used terms in business; they are often stretched to mean everything—and end up meaning nothing. But as the experiences of companies like Dell and Wal-Mart show, these are concepts with enormous practical value. It's true that any attempt to draw sharp boundaries around abstract terms involves some arbitrary choices. But unless we're willing to draw the line somewhere, these concepts will remain confusing and difficult to use. Definition brings clarity. And when it comes to concepts that are so fundamental to performance, no organization can afford fuzzy thinking.

Originally published in May 2002. Reprint R0205F

Notes

1. James C. Collins and Jerry I. Porras, *Built to Last* (HarperCollins, 1994).
2. "Meg Whitman at eBay Inc. (A)," HBS case no. 9-400-035.
3. "Wal-Mart Stores, Inc.," HBS case no. 9-794-024.

Reinventing Your Business Model

by Mark W. Johnson, Clayton M. Christensen, and Henning Kagermann

IN 2003, APPLE INTRODUCED the iPod with the iTunes store, revolutionizing portable entertainment, creating a new market, and transforming the company. In just three years, the iPod/iTunes combination became a nearly $10 billion product, accounting for almost 50% of Apple's revenue. Apple's market capitalization catapulted from around $1 billion in early 2003 to over $150 billion by late 2007.

This success story is well known; what's less well known is that Apple was not the first to bring digital music players to market. A company called Diamond Multimedia introduced the Rio in 1998. Another firm, Best Data, introduced the Cabo 64 in 2000. Both products worked well and were portable and stylish. So why did the iPod, rather than the Rio or Cabo, succeed?

Apple did something far smarter than take a good technology and wrap it in a snazzy design. It took a good technology and wrapped it in a great business model. Apple's true innovation was to make downloading digital music easy and convenient. To do that, the company built a groundbreaking business model that combined hardware, software, and service. This approach worked like Gillette's famous blades-and-razor model in reverse: Apple essentially gave away the "blades" (low-margin iTunes music) to lock in purchase of the "razor" (the high-margin iPod). That model defined value in a new way and provided game-changing convenience to the consumer.

Business model innovations have reshaped entire industries and redistributed billions of dollars of value. Retail discounters such as Wal-Mart and Target, which entered the market with pioneering business models, now account for 75% of the total valuation of the retail sector. Low-cost U.S. airlines grew from a blip on the radar screen to 55% of the market value of all carriers. Fully 11 of the 27 companies born in the last quarter century that grew their way into the *Fortune* 500 in the past 10 years did so through business model innovation.

Stories of business model innovation from well-established companies like Apple, however, are rare. An analysis of major innovations within existing corporations in the past decade shows that precious few have been business-model related. And a recent American Management Association study determined that no more than 10% of innovation investment at global companies is focused on developing new business models.

Yet everyone's talking about it. A 2005 survey by the Economist Intelligence Unit reported that over 50% of executives believe business model innovation will become even more important for success than product or service innovation. A 2008 IBM survey of corporate CEOs echoed these results. Nearly all of the CEOs polled reported the need to adapt their business models; more than two-thirds said that extensive changes were required. And in these tough economic times, some CEOs are already looking to business model innovation to address permanent shifts in their market landscapes.

Senior managers at incumbent companies thus confront a frustrating question: Why is it so difficult to pull off the new growth that business model innovation can bring? Our research suggests two problems. The first is a lack of definition: Very little formal study has been done into the dynamics and processes of business model development. Second, few companies understand their existing business model well enough—the premise behind its development, its natural interdependencies, and its strengths and limitations. So they don't know when they can leverage their core business and when success requires a new business model.

Idea in Brief

When Apple introduced the iPod, it did something far smarter than wrap a good technology in a snazzy design. It wrapped a good technology in a great business model. Combining hardware, software, and service, the model provided game-changing convenience for consumers *and* record-breaking profits for Apple.

Great business models can reshape industries and drive spectacular growth. Yet many companies find business-model innovation difficult. Managers don't understand their existing model well enough to know when it needs changing—or how.

To determine whether your firm should alter its business model, Johnson, Christensen, and Kagermann advise these steps:

1. Articulate what makes your existing model successful. For example, what customer problem does it solve? How does it make money for your firm?

2. Watch for signals that your model needs changing, such as tough new competitors on the horizon.

3. Decide whether reinventing your model is worth the effort. The answer's yes only if the new model changes the industry or market.

After tackling these problems with dozens of companies, we have found that new business models often look unattractive to internal and external stakeholders—at the outset. To see past the borders of what is and into the land of the new, companies need a road map.

Ours consists of three simple steps. The first is to realize that success starts by not thinking about business models at all. It starts with thinking about the opportunity to satisfy a real customer who needs a job done. The second step is to construct a blueprint laying out how your company will fulfill that need at a profit. In our model, that plan has four elements. The third is to compare that model to your existing model to see how much you'd have to change it to capture the opportunity. Once you do, you will know if you can use your existing model and organization or need to separate out a new unit to execute a new model. Every successful company is already fulfilling a real customer need with an effective business model, whether that model is explicitly understood or not. Let's take a look at what that entails.

Idea in Practice

Understand Your Current Business Model

A successful model has these components:

- **Customer value proposition.** The model helps customers perform a specific "job" that alternative offerings don't address.

  Example: MinuteClinics enable people to visit a doctor's office without appointments by making nurse practitioners available to treat minor health issues.

- **Profit formula.** The model generates value for your company through factors such as revenue model, cost structure, margins, and inventory turnover.

  Example: The Tata Group's inexpensive car, the Nano, is profitable because the company has reduced many cost structure elements, accepted lower-than-standard gross margins, and sold the Nano in large volumes to its target market: first-time car buyers in emerging markets.

- **Key resources and processes.** Your company has the people, technology, products, facilities, equipment, and brand required to deliver the value proposition to your targeted customers. And it has processes (training, manufacturing, service) to leverage those resources.

  Example: For Tata Motors to fulfill the requirements of the Nano's profit formula, it had to reconceive how a car is designed, manufactured, and distributed. It redefined its supplier strategy, choosing to outsource a remarkable 85% of the Nano's components and to use nearly 60% fewer vendors than normal to reduce transaction costs.

Identify When a New Model May Be Needed

These circumstances often require business model change:

Business Model: A Definition

A business model, from our point of view, consists of four interlocking elements that, taken together, create and deliver value. The most important to get right, by far, is the first.

Customer value proposition (CVP)

A successful company is one that has found a way to create value for customers—that is, a way to help customers get an important job

An *opportunity* to . . .	Example
Address needs of large groups who find existing solutions too expensive or complicated.	The Nano's goal is to open car ownership to low-income consumers in emerging markets.
Capitalize on new technology, or leverage existing technologies in new markets.	A company develops a commercial application for a technology originally developed for military use.
Bring a job-to-be-done focus where it doesn't exist.	FedEx focused on performing customers' unmet "job": Receive packages faster and more reliably than any other service could.

A *need* to . . .	Example
Fend off low-end disruptors.	Mini-mills threatened the integrated steel mills a generation ago by making steel at significantly lower prices.
Respond to shifts in competition.	Power-tool maker Hilti switched from selling to renting its tools in part because "good enough" low-end entrants had begun chipping away at the market for selling high-quality tools.

done. By "job" we mean a fundamental problem in a given situation that needs a solution. Once we understand the job and all its dimensions, including the full process for how to get it done, we can design the offering. The more important the job is to the customer, the lower the level of customer satisfaction with current options for getting the job done, and the better your solution is than existing alternatives at getting the job done (and, of course, the lower the price), the greater the CVP. Opportunities for creating a CVP are at their most potent, we have found, when alternative products and services have not been designed with the real job in mind and you can design an offering that gets that job—and only that job—done perfectly. We'll come back to that point later.

Profit formula

The profit formula is the blueprint that defines how the company creates value for itself while providing value to the customer. It consists of the following:

- *Revenue model:* price x volume

- *Cost structure:* direct costs, indirect costs, economies of scale. Cost structure will be predominantly driven by the cost of the key resources required by the business model.

- *Margin model:* given the expected volume and cost structure, the contribution needed from each transaction to achieve desired profits.

- *Resource velocity:* how fast we need to turn over inventory, fixed assets, and other assets—and, overall, how well we need to utilize resources—to support our expected volume and achieve our anticipated profits.

People often think the terms "profit formulas" and "business models" are interchangeable. But how you make a profit is only one piece of the model. We've found it most useful to start by setting the price required to deliver the CVP and then work backwards from there to determine what the variable costs and gross margins must be. This then determines what the scale and resource velocity needs to be to achieve the desired profits.

Key resources

The key resources are assets such as the people, technology, products, facilities, equipment, channels, and brand required to deliver the value proposition to the targeted customer. The focus here is on the *key* elements that create value for the customer and the company, and the way those elements interact. (Every company also has generic resources that do not create competitive differentiation.)

Key processes
Successful companies have operational and managerial processes that allow them to deliver value in a way they can successfully repeat and increase in scale. These may include such recurrent tasks as training, development, manufacturing, budgeting, planning, sales, and service. Key processes also include a company's rules, metrics, and norms.

These four elements form the building blocks of any business. The customer value proposition and the profit formula define value for the customer and the company, respectively; key resources and key processes describe how that value will be delivered to both the customer and the company.

As simple as this framework may seem, its power lies in the complex interdependencies of its parts. Major changes to any of these four elements affect the others and the whole. Successful businesses devise a more or less stable system in which these elements bond to one another in consistent and complementary ways.

How Great Models Are Built

To illustrate the elements of our business model framework, we will look at what's behind two companies' game-changing business model innovations.

Creating a customer value proposition
It's not possible to invent or reinvent a business model without first identifying a clear customer value proposition. Often, it starts as a quite simple realization. Imagine, for a moment, that you are standing on a Mumbai road on a rainy day. You notice the large number of motor scooters snaking precariously in and out around the cars. As you look more closely, you see that most bear whole families—both parents and several children. Your first thought might be "That's

The Elements of a Successful
Business Model

EVERY SUCCESSFUL COMPANY ALREADY operates according to an effective business model. By systematically identifying all of its constituent parts, executives can understand how the model fulfills a potent value proposition in a profitable way using certain key resources and key processes. With that understanding, they can then judge how well the same model could be used to fulfill a radically different CVP—and what they'd need to do to construct a new one, if need be, to capitalize on that opportunity.

Customer Value Proposition (CVP)
- **Target customer**
- **Job to be done** to solve an important problem or fulfill an important need for the target customer
- **Offering**, which satisfies the problem or fulfills the need. This is defined not only by what is sold but also by how it's sold.

PROFIT FORMULA

- **Revenue model** How much money can be made: price x volume. Volume can be thought of in terms of market size, purchase frequency, ancillary sales, etc.

- **Cost structure** How costs are allocated: includes cost of key assets, direct costs, indirect costs, economies of scale.

- **Margin model** How much each transaction should net to achieve desired profit levels.

- **Resource velocity** How quickly resources need to be used to support target volume. Includes lead times, throughput, inventory turns, asset utilization, and so on.

KEY RESOURCES
needed to deliver the customer value proposition profitably. Might include:
- **People**
- **Technology, products**
- **Equipment**
- **Information**
- **Channels**
- **Partnerships, alliances**
- **Brand**

KEY PROCESSES, as well as rules, metrics, and norms, that make the profitable delivery of the customer value proposition repeatable and scalable. Might include:

- **Processes:** design, product development, sourcing, manufacturing, marketing, hiring and training, IT

- **Rules and metrics:** margin requirements for investment, credit terms, lead times, supplier terms

- **Norms:** opportunity size needed for investment, approach to customers and channels

crazy!" or "That's the way it is in developing countries—people get by as best they can."

When Ratan Tata of Tata Group looked out over this scene, he saw a critical job to be done: providing a safer alternative for scooter families. He understood that the cheapest car available in India cost easily five times what a scooter did and that many of these families could not afford one. Offering an affordable, safer, all-weather alternative for scooter families was a powerful value proposition, one with the potential to reach tens of millions of people who were not yet part of the car-buying market. Ratan Tata also recognized that Tata Motors' business model could not be used to develop such a product at the needed price point.

At the other end of the market spectrum, Hilti, a Liechtenstein-based manufacturer of high-end power tools for the construction industry, reconsidered the real job to be done for many of its current customers. A contractor makes money by finishing projects; if the required tools aren't available and functioning properly, the job doesn't get done. Contractors don't make money by *owning* tools; they make it by using them as efficiently as possible. Hilti could help contractors get the job done by selling tool *use* instead of the tools themselves—managing its customers' tool inventory by providing the best tool at the right time and quickly furnishing tool repairs, replacements, and upgrades, all for a monthly fee. To deliver on that value proposition, the company needed to create a fleet-management program for tools and in the process shift its focus from manufacturing and distribution to service. That meant Hilti had to construct a new profit formula and develop new resources and new processes.

The most important attribute of a customer value proposition is its precision: how perfectly it nails the customer job to be done—and nothing else. But such precision is often the most difficult thing to achieve. Companies trying to create the new often neglect to focus on *one* job; they dilute their efforts by attempting to do lots of things. In doing lots of things, they do nothing *really* well.

One way to generate a precise customer value proposition is to think about the four most common barriers keeping people from

Hilti Sidesteps Commoditization

HILTI IS CAPITALIZING ON a game-changing opportunity to increase profitability by turning products into a service. Rather than sell tools (at lower and lower prices), it's selling a "just-the-tool-you-need-when-you-need-it, no-repair-or-storage-hassles" service. Such a radical change in customer value proposition required a shift in all parts of its business model.

Traditional power tool company		Hilti's tool fleet management service
Sales of industrial and professional power tools and accessories	**Customer value proposition**	Leasing a comprehensive fleet of tools to increase contractors's on-site productivity
Low margins, high inventory turnover	**Profit formula**	Higher margins; asset heavy; monthly payments for tool maintenance, repair, and replacement
Distribution channel, low-cost manufacturing plants in developing countries, R&D	**Key resources and processes**	Strong direct-sales approach, contract management, IT systems for inventory management and repair, warehousing

getting particular jobs done: insufficient wealth, access, skill, or time. Software maker Intuit devised QuickBooks to fulfill small-business owners' need to avoid running out of cash. By fulfilling that job with greatly simplified accounting software, Intuit broke the *skills barrier* that kept untrained small-business owners from using more-complicated accounting packages. MinuteClinic, the drugstore-based basic health care provider, broke the *time barrier* that kept people from visiting a doctor's office with minor health issues by making nurse practitioners available without appointments.

Designing a profit formula

Ratan Tata knew the only way to get families off their scooters and into cars would be to break the *wealth barrier* by drastically decreasing the price of the car. "What if I can change the game and make a car for one lakh?" Tata wondered, envisioning a price point of around US$2,500, less than half the price of the cheapest car available. This, of course, had dramatic ramifications for the profit formula: It required both a significant drop in gross margins and a radical reduction in many elements of the cost structure. He knew, however, he could still make money if he could increase sales volume dramatically, and he knew that his target base of consumers was potentially huge.

For Hilti, moving to a contract management program required shifting assets from customers' balance sheets to its own and generating revenue through a lease/subscription model. For a monthly fee, customers could have a full complement of tools at their fingertips, with repair and maintenance included. This would require a fundamental shift in all major components of the profit formula: the revenue stream (pricing, the staging of payments, and how to think about volume), the cost structure (including added sales development and contract management costs), and the supporting margins and transaction velocity.

Identifying key resources and processes

Having articulated the value proposition for both the customer and the business, companies must then consider the key resources and processes needed to deliver that value. For a professional services firm, for example, the key resources are generally its people, and the key processes are naturally people related (training and development, for instance). For a packaged goods company, strong brands and well-selected channel retailers might be the key resources, and associated brand-building and channel-management processes among the critical processes.

Oftentimes, it's not the individual resources and processes that make the difference but their relationship to one another. Companies will almost always need to integrate their key resources and processes in a unique way to get a job done perfectly for a set of customers. When they do, they almost always create enduring competitive advantage. Focusing first on the value proposition and the profit formula makes clear how those resources and processes need to interrelate. For example, most general hospitals offer a value proposition that might be described as, "We'll do anything for anybody." Being all things to all people requires these hospitals to have a vast collection of resources (specialists, equipment, and so on) that can't be knit together in any proprietary way. The result is not just a lack of differentiation but dissatisfaction.

By contrast, a hospital that focuses on a specific value proposition can integrate its resources and processes in a unique way that delights customers. National Jewish Health in Denver, for example, is organized around a focused value proposition we'd characterize as, "If you have a disease of the pulmonary system, bring it here. We'll define its root cause and prescribe an effective therapy." Narrowing its focus has allowed National Jewish to develop processes that integrate the ways in which its specialists and specialized equipment work together.

For Tata Motors to fulfill the requirements of its customer value proposition and profit formula for the Nano, it had to reconceive how a car is designed, manufactured, and distributed. Tata built a small team of fairly young engineers who would not, like the company's more-experienced designers, be influenced and constrained in their thinking by the automaker's existing profit formulas. This team dramatically minimized the number of parts in the vehicle, resulting in a significant cost saving. Tata also reconceived its supplier strategy, choosing to outsource a remarkable 85% of the Nano's components and use nearly 60% fewer vendors than normal to reduce transaction costs and achieve better economies of scale.

At the other end of the manufacturing line, Tata is envisioning an entirely new way of assembling and distributing its cars. The ultimate plan is to ship the modular components of the vehicles to a combined network of company-owned and independent entrepreneur-owned assembly plants, which will build them to order. The Nano will be designed, built, distributed, and serviced in a radically new way—one that could not be accomplished without a new business model. And while the jury is still out, Ratan Tata may solve a traffic safety problem in the process.

For Hilti, the greatest challenge lay in training its sales representatives to do a thoroughly new task. Fleet management is not a half-hour sale; it takes days, weeks, even months of meetings to persuade customers to buy a program instead of a product. Suddenly, field reps accustomed to dealing with crew leaders and on-site purchasing managers in mobile trailers found themselves staring down CEOs and CFOs across conference tables.

Additionally, leasing required new resources—new people, more robust IT systems, and other new technologies—to design and develop the appropriate packages and then come to an agreement on monthly payments. Hilti needed a process for maintaining large arsenals of tools more inexpensively and effectively than its customers had. This required warehousing, an inventory management system, and a supply of replacement tools. On the customer management side, Hilti developed a website that enabled construction managers to view all the tools in their fleet and their usage rates. With that information readily available, the managers could easily handle the cost accounting associated with those assets.

Rules, norms, and metrics are often the last element to emerge in a developing business model. They may not be fully envisioned until the new product or service has been road tested. Nor should they be. Business models need to have the flexibility to change in their early years.

When a New Business Model Is Needed

Established companies should not undertake business-model innovation lightly. They can often create new products that disrupt competitors without fundamentally changing their own business model. Procter & Gamble, for example, developed a number of what it calls "disruptive market innovations" with such products as the Swiffer disposable mop and duster and Febreze, a new kind of air freshener. Both innovations built on P&G's existing business model and its established dominance in household consumables.

There are clearly times, however, when creating new growth requires venturing not only into unknown market territory but also into unknown business model territory. When? The short answer is "When significant changes are needed to all four elements of your existing model." But it's not always that simple. Management judgment is clearly required. That said, we have observed five strategic circumstances that often require business model change:

1. The opportunity to address through disruptive innovation the needs of large groups of potential customers who are shut out of a market entirely because existing solutions are too expensive or complicated for them. This includes the opportunity to democratize products in emerging markets (or reach the bottom of the pyramid), as Tata's Nano does.

2. The opportunity to capitalize on a brand-new technology by wrapping a new business model around it (Apple and MP3 players) or the opportunity to leverage a tested technology by bringing it to a whole new market (say, by offering military technologies in the commercial space or vice versa).

3. The opportunity to bring a job-to-be-done focus where one does not yet exist. That's common in industries where companies focus on products or customer segments, which leads them to refine existing products more and more, increasing commoditization over time. A jobs focus allows companies to redefine industry profitability. For example, when FedEx entered the package delivery market, it did not try to compete through lower prices or better marketing. Instead, it concentrated on fulfilling an entirely unmet customer need to receive packages far, far faster, and more reliably, than any service then could. To do so, it had to integrate its key processes and resources in a vastly more efficient way. The business model that resulted from this job-to-be-done emphasis gave FedEx a significant competitive advantage that took UPS many years to copy.

4. The need to fend off low-end disrupters. If the Nano is successful, it will threaten other automobile makers, much as minimills threatened the integrated steel mills a generation ago by making steel at significantly lower cost.

5. The need to respond to a shifting basis of competition. Inevitably, what defines an acceptable solution in a market will change over time, leading core market segments to commoditize. Hilti needed to change its business model in part because of lower global manufacturing costs; "good enough" low-end entrants had begun chipping away at the market for high-quality power tools.

Of course, companies should not pursue business model reinvention unless they are confident that the opportunity is large enough to warrant the effort. And, there's really no point in instituting a new business model unless it's not only new to the company but in some way new or game-changing to the industry or market. To do otherwise would be a waste of time and money.

These questions will help you evaluate whether the challenge of business model innovation will yield acceptable results. Answering "yes" to all four greatly increases the odds of successful execution:

- Can you nail the job with a focused, compelling customer value proposition?

- Can you devise a model in which all the elements—the customer value proposition, the profit formula, the key resources, and the key processes—work together to get the job done in the most efficient way possible?

- Can you create a new business development process unfettered by the often negative influences of your core business?

- Will the new business model disrupt competitors?

Creating a new model for a new business does not mean the current model is threatened or should be changed. A new model often reinforces and complements the core business, as Dow Corning discovered.

Dow Corning Embraces the Low End

TRADITIONALLY HIGH-MARGIN DOW CORNING found new opportunities in low-margin offerings by setting up a separate business unit that operates in an entirely different way. By fundamentally differentiating its low-end and high-end offerings, the company avoided cannibalizing its traditional business even as it found new profits at the low end.

Established business		New business unit
Customized solutions, negotiated contracts	**Customer value proposition**	No frills, bulk prices, sold through the internet
High-margin, high-overhead retail prices pay for value-added services	**Profit formula**	Spot-market pricing, low overhead to accommodate lower margins, high throughput
R&D, sales, and services orientation	**Key resources and processes**	IT system, lowest-cost processes, maximum automation

How Dow Corning Got Out of Its Own Way

When business model innovation is clearly called for, success lies not only in getting the model right but also in making sure the incumbent business doesn't in some way prevent the new model from creating value or thriving. That was a problem for Dow Corning when it built a new business unit—with a new profit formula—from scratch.

For many years, Dow Corning had sold thousands of silicone-based products and provided sophisticated technical services to an array of industries. After years of profitable growth, however, a number of product areas were stagnating. A strategic review uncovered a critical insight: Its low-end product segment was commoditizing. Many customers experienced in silicone application no longer needed technical services; they needed basic products at low prices. This shift created an opportunity for growth, but to exploit that opportunity Dow Corning had to figure out a way to serve these customers with a lower-priced product. The problem was that both

When the Old Model Will Work

YOU DON'T ALWAYS NEED a new business model to capitalize on a game-changing opportunity. Sometimes, as P&G did with its Swiffer, a company finds that its current model is revolutionary in a new market. When will the old model do? When you can fulfill the new customer value proposition:

- With your current profit formula

- Using most, if not all, of your current key resources and processes

- Using the same core metrics, rules, and norms you now use to run your business

the business model and the culture were built on high-priced, innovative product and service packages. In 2002, in pursuit of what was essentially a commodity business for low-end customers, Dow Corning CEO Gary Anderson asked executive Don Sheets to form a team to start a new business.

The team began by formulating a customer value proposition that it believed would fulfill the job to be done for these price-driven customers. It determined that the price point had to drop 15% (which for a commoditizing material was a huge reduction). As the team analyzed what that new customer value proposition would require, it realized reaching that point was going to take a lot more than merely eliminating services. Dramatic price reduction would call for a different profit formula with a fundamentally lower cost structure, which depended heavily on developing a new IT system. To sell more products faster, the company would need to use the internet to automate processes and reduce overhead as much as possible.

Breaking the rules

As a mature and successful company, Dow Corning was full of highly trained employees used to delivering its high-touch, customized value proposition. To automate, the new business would have to be far more standardized, which meant instituting different and, overall, much stricter rules. For example, order sizes would be limited to a few, larger-volume options; order lead times would fall between two and four weeks (exceptions would cost extra); and credit terms would be fixed. There would be charges if a purchaser required customer service. The writing was on the wall: The new venture would be low-touch, self-service, and standardized. To succeed, Dow Corning would have to break the rules that had previously guided its success.

Sheets next had to determine whether this new venture, with its new rules, could succeed within the confines of Dow Corning's core enterprise. He set up an experimental war game to test how existing staff and systems would react to the requirements of the new customer value proposition. He got crushed as entrenched habits and existing processes thwarted any attempt to change the game. It became clear that the corporate antibodies would kill the initiative before it got off the ground. The way forward was clear: The new venture had to be free from existing rules and free to decide what rules would be appropriate in order for the new commodity line of business to thrive. To nurture the opportunity—and also protect the existing model—a new business unit with a new brand identity was needed. Xiameter was born.

Identifying new competencies
Following the articulation of the new customer value proposition and new profit formula, the Xiameter team focused on the new competencies it would need, its key resources and processes. Information technology, just a small part of Dow Corning's core competencies at that time, emerged as an essential part of the now web-enabled business. Xiameter also needed employees who could make smart decisions very quickly and who would thrive in a fast-changing environment, filled initially with lots of ambiguity. Clearly, new abilities would have to be brought into the business.

Although Xiameter would be established and run as a separate business unit, Don Sheets and the Xiameter team did not want to give up the incumbency advantage that deep knowledge of the industry and of their own products gave them. The challenge was to tap into the expertise without importing the old-rules mind-set.

What Rules, Norms, and Metrics Are Standing in Your Way?

IN ANY BUSINESS, a fundamental understanding of the core model often fades into the mists of institutional memory, but it lives on in rules, norms, and metrics put in place to protect the status quo (for example, "Gross margins must be at 40%"). They are the first line of defense against any new model's taking root in an existing enterprise.

Financial

- Gross margins
- Opportunity size
- Unit pricing
- Unit margin
- Time to breakeven
- Net present value calculations
- Fixed cost investment
- Credit items

Operational

- End-product quality
- Supplier quality
- Owned versus outsourced manufacturing
- Customer service
- Channels
- Lead times
- Throughput

Other

- Pricing
- Performance demands
- Product-development life cycles
- Basis for individuals' rewards and incentives
- Brand parameters

Sheets conducted a focused HR search within Dow Corning for risk takers. During the interview process, when he came across candidates with the right skills, he asked them to take the job on the spot, before they left the room. This approach allowed him to cherry-pick those who could make snap decisions and take big risks.

Business Model Analogies

by Mark Johnson

Type	Example	Description
Affinity club	MBNA	Partner with membership associations and other affinity groups to offer a product exclusively to its members, exchanging royalties for access to a larger customer base.
Automation-enabled services	Betterment, IBM Watson	Harness software that automates processes previously requiring human labor and cognition to reduce operating costs.
Brokerage	Century 21, Orbitz	Bring together and facilitate transactions between buyers and sellers, charging a fee for each successful transaction.
Bundling	Fast-food value meals, iPod/iTunes	Make purchasing simple and more complete by packaging related products together.
Crowdsourcing	Wikipedia, YouTube	Outsource tasks to a broad group that contributes content for free in exchange for access to other users' content.
Data-into-assets	Waze, Facebook	Use data management and analysis processes to capture value from having access to or ownership of data.
Digital platforms	OpenTable, Airbnb, Uber	Enable value-creating interactions between external producers and consumers through open, participative infrastructure with set governance conditions.
Disintermediation	Dell, WebMD	Deliver directly to the customer a product or service that has traditionally gone through an intermediary.
Fractionalization	Time-sharing condos, NetJets	Allow users to own part of a product or service but enjoy many of the benefits of full ownership at a fraction of the price.
Freemium	Spotify, LinkedIn, Dropbox	Offer basic services for free but charge for upgraded or premium services.
Leasing	Luxury cars, Xerox, MachineryLink	Make high-margin, high-cost products affordable by having the customer rent rather than buy them.

Type	Example	Description
Low-touch	Southwest, Walmart, Xiameter	Offer low-price, low-service version of a traditionally high-end offering.
Negative operating cycle	Amazon	Generate high profits by maintaining low inventory and having the customer pay up front for a product or service to be delivered in the future.
Pay-as-you-go	Amazon Web Services, car2go	Charge the customer for metered services based on actual usage rates.
Razors/blades	Gillette, personal printers	Offer the higher-margin "razors" for low or no cost to make profits by selling high-volume, low-margin "blades."
Reverse razors/ blades	iPod/iTunes, Amazon Kindle	Offer the low-margin "blades" at no or low cost to encourage sales of the higher-margin "razors."
Product-to-service	IBM, Hilti, Zipcar	Rather than sell the products outright, sell the service the product performs.
Standardization	MinuteClinic	Provide lower-cost standardized solution to problems that once could be addressed through high-cost customized products or services.
Subscription club	Netflix, Five Four Club, Dollar Shave Club	Charge the customer a subscription fee to gain access to a product or service.
User communities	Angie's List	Grant members access to a network, generating revenue through membership fees and advertisements.

Source: from Mark W. Johnson, *Reinvent Your Business Model* (Boston: Harvard Business Review Press, 2018), 145–146.

The secret sauce: patience

Successful new businesses typically revise their business models four times or so on the road to profitability. While a well-considered business-model-innovation process can often shorten this cycle, successful incumbents must tolerate initial failure and grasp the need for course correction. In effect, companies have to focus on learning and adjusting as much as on executing. We recommend companies with new business models be patient for growth (to allow the market opportunity to unfold) but impatient for profit (as an early validation that the model works). A profitable business is the best early indication of a viable model.

Accordingly, to allow for the trial and error that naturally accompanies the creation of the new while also constructing a development cycle that would produce results and demonstrate feasibility with minimal resource outlay, Dow Corning kept the scale of Xiameter's operation small but developed an aggressive timetable for launch and set the goal of becoming profitable by the end of year one.

Xiameter paid back Dow Corning's investment in just three months and went on to become a major, transformative success. Beforehand, Dow Corning had had no online sales component; now 30% of sales originate online, nearly three times the industry average. Most of these customers are new to the company. Far from cannibalizing existing customers, Xiameter has actually supported the main business, allowing Dow Corning's salespeople to more easily enforce premium pricing for their core offerings while providing a viable alternative for the price-conscious.

Established companies' attempts at transformative growth typically spring from product or technology innovations. Their efforts are often characterized by prolonged development cycles and fitful attempts to find a market. As the Apple iPod story that opened this article suggests, truly transformative businesses are never exclusively about the discovery and commercialization of a great technology. Their success comes from enveloping the new technology in an appropriate, powerful business model.

Bob Higgins, the founder and general partner of Highland Capital Partners, has seen his share of venture success and failure in his 20 years in the industry. He sums up the importance and power of business model innovation this way: "I think historically where we [venture capitalists] fail is when we back technology. Where we succeed is when we back new business models."

Originally published in December 2008. Reprint R0812C

When Your Business Model Is in Trouble

An interview with Rita Gunther McGrath. *by Sarah Cliffe*

Columbia Business School professor **RITA GUNTHER McGRATH** *studies strategy in highly uncertain, volatile environments. She spoke recently with HBR executive editor Sarah Cliffe about how to recognize an oncoming crisis—and seize opportunities to get ahead of competitors.*

HBR: *Why is there so much interest in business model innovation right now?*

McGrath: I see three main reasons. The first is the increasing speed of everything. Product life cycles and design cycles are getting shorter. When the pace of change gets faster, people realize that they need to look for the next big thing. The second issue is inter-industry competition. Competition is coming from unexpected places. Who could have anticipated that the iPad's success would put all kinds of display devices—like electronic photo frames—out of business? And the third trend is disruptions from business models that offer better customer experiences instead of simply products. Traditional toy retailers are struggling, but Build-a-Bear gets people to pay good money to provide free labor and make their product themselves. Maxine Clark, the entrepreneur who thought that up, was brilliant!

Which industries are facing the biggest disruptions?

You'd do better to ask which industries are *not* being disrupted. Oil and gas are probably stable. Some consumer packaged goods are, too. But if you don't have strong barriers to entry or you're up against shifts in technology or regulation, you're going to face new kinds of competition. It's just so easy for someone to come after you once you've demonstrated that a market exists.

What are the signs that a business model is running out of gas?

The first clear stage is when next-generation innovations offer smaller and smaller improvements. If your people have trouble thinking of new ways to enhance your offering, that's a sign. Second, you hear customers saying that new alternatives are increasingly acceptable to them. And finally, the problem starts to show up in your financial numbers or other performance indicators.

There's always very early evidence that a business model is in trouble, but it usually gets ignored or dismissed. That's because at most companies the people at the top got there because of their success with the current model—so they have very few incentives to question its durability. So you get a denial reaction initially, followed by desperate attempts to eke just a little more time out of the existing model. The recognition that things must change happens only when it is far too late, and then change is much more painful than it had to be.

Are there any business models—like the experience providers you mentioned—that are on their way up?

Some business models are more powerful than others. Basically, you should look for models that create customer stickiness or loyalty or barriers to entry. Anything that gets automatically renewed gives you a certain amount of stickiness, especially if the customer has to work to change providers. Anyone who has ever tried to move from one cell phone service to another while holding on to their phone number has experienced this—it's a time-consuming hassle. One reason companies are so motivated to get you to manage your accounts online with them is that once you do, it takes serious work

Idea in Brief

With product life cycles growing ever shorter and competition cropping up in unexpected places, nearly every industry is facing disruption. How can you tell if your business model is running out of gas? For starters, if your next-generation innovations provide smaller and smaller improvements and your people have trouble thinking of new ways to enhance your offering. Pay heed to the signs and start experimenting with several new options until you find one that will turn your threat into an opportunity.

to discontinue the relationship. Anything where your service is embedded into the clients' service, so that clients depend on you to provide critical steps in their processes, is sticky. IBM, for example, gains this advantage when it takes over portions of a client's computing processes. In those models customers aren't going to abandon you unless you get arrogant or greedy. Then there are the platform models. Microsoft is a classic example. It doesn't just sell application software—it makes a lot of money licensing software platforms to other organizations. Platforms allow you to charge more and to hold on to an advantage for a long time.

What models should be avoided?

Those where the customer buys something once and is done. Also—and this is a bigger problem than you'd think—make sure you have a revenue model! People are starting businesses that give away a lot for free. Sometimes that's OK if you can experiment at low cost or you have patient venture capitalists. But you really want a model with a clear path to monetization.

Say you're meeting with a company that wants to reinvent its model. Who should be in the room?

Wait, back up. First you need to have processes in place that cause you to challenge the existing assumptions in your model. For example, Andrea Jung ran Avon very successfully, but then it got into big trouble. One of her advisers suggested that if things were going so badly that she was about to lose her job, maybe she should fire herself on Friday afternoon and rehire herself on Monday morning, and then look at everything in the company with fresh eyes. This led Jung to make some very tough choices—cutting 25% of her own handpicked managers, changing marketing programs, and reversing course on investments she had previously advocated.

So the first step is to build mechanisms that cause you to reexamine your assumptions. One question I encourage people to ask is, What data would lead us to make a different decision? Be sure you're not getting only information that confirms your preexisting beliefs. Then you can think about what nontraditional information to seek out. You need to get unfiltered information by talking to customers directly and by going through the experiences they go through. You want to get out of the room, in other words. Do your own version of *Undercover Boss* and see what insights you can get. I'll never forget an experience I had with classroom participants from a wireless telecom company that was regularly criticized for poor network coverage. When I asked them, "Why are your senior managers not bothered by this?" they said, "We know where their offices are, what routes they take to work, and where they go on weekends. We make sure the network is working in those places." This insulation from reality can be deadly. You need direct contact with the truth.

Once you've done all that, then you can bring together a diverse group—people who know something about the technology, people who understand customer needs, people who have a longer view of where things might be evolving—and develop hypotheses about the areas where you should experiment.

How do you choose among possible experiments to invest in?

You need a portfolio of opportunities. I believe in investing in several options: Some will pay off, and some won't. Some of them might be mutually exclusive. Verizon, for example, knew that landline telephones were disappearing. A lot of companies would have just milked that business for the cash cow that it was, but Ivan Seidenberg took out investments in four or five mutually exclusive networking technologies and let them run until it became clear which one would be dominant. Then he invested heavily in that technology and shut the others down. Most companies don't do that. Instead, they fund the one project with the best numbers.

What's the right pace for change if you're still making good money from your existing businesses and you've got this portfolio of new investments?

That's one of the most difficult issues—I wish I had a clear answer for you. The best attempt we've made is to calculate what we call bare-bones net present values: Make some guesses about when the cash flows from new businesses will come onstream. Then figure out how to get cash out of your declining businesses or find another way to benefit from them. For instance, you can license technology to others who still have an interest in it. You can continue to run the business but out-source its operations to a lower-cost provider. That transition period is tough, but it's good to spend time thinking through the issues.

I'm guessing that shareholders aren't especially patient with the messiness of those transitions.

You've got that right. If a company needs to get out of a business—take write-offs, get rid of assets—the Street doesn't like that. But private equity firms like it a lot. A fair number of firms going through a big business model change right now are partially or wholly in the hands of private equity players, and I don't think that's an accident. Some of the more-enlightened companies I've spoken with have talked about recruiting investors who are willing to be patient.

Do family-controlled businesses have a better record of patient investing?

Without a doubt. Bose recently released a product called Video-Wave, which creates a high-end home theater. The company spent five years developing it. That's a long time to wait for new revenues. But the people at Bose think that because they had the patience to get it right, the premium-price advantage and the business model will last. They can invest in deep science because they've maintained private ownership for a long, long time. They've looked at the stock market and said, "Nope, not for us."

I suspect we'll see a different approach to investment coming out of this wave of business model changes. Think about it: Do the capital markets operate in a way that encourages companies to make the right kinds of decisions as they face large-scale change? I'm dubious.

Anything else companies can do to turn threats to their models into opportunities?

When companies don't respond to business model challenges, it's usually because of internally generated problems like the lack of incentives I mentioned earlier and too much distance from the customer. I would encourage managers to think about what internal issues they should be tackling right now. Because when everything's fine, when your model is chugging along and you're doing your day job, it's easy to ignore those issues. Organizations have powerful inertia. It's like kids. At night, can you get them to go to bed? No. In the morning, can you get them to wake up? No. They want to keep doing whatever it is they're doing. Organizations are just the same.

Originally published in January–February 2011. Reprint R1101F

Four Paths to Business Model Innovation

by Karan Girotra and Serguei Netessine

BUSINESS MODEL INNOVATION is a wonderful thing. At its simplest, it demands neither new technologies nor the creation of brand-new markets: It's about delivering *existing* products that are produced by *existing* technologies to *existing* markets. And because it often involves changes invisible to the outside world, it can bring advantages that are hard to copy.

The challenge is defining what business model innovation actually entails. Without a framework for identifying opportunities, it is hard to be systematic about the process, which explains why it is generally done on an ad hoc basis. As a result, many companies miss out on inexpensive ways to improve their profitability and productivity.

In the following pages we present a framework to help managers take business model innovation to the level of a reliable and improvable discipline. Drawing on the idea that any business model is essentially a set of key decisions that collectively determine how a business earns its revenue, incurs its costs, and manages its risks, we view innovations to the model as changes to those decisions: *what* your offerings will be, *when* decisions are made, *who* makes them, and *why*. Successful changes along these dimensions improve the company's combination of revenue, costs, and risks.

What Mix of Products or Services Should You Offer?

Uncertain demand is a challenge all businesses face and is in most cases their major source of risk. One way to reduce that risk is to make changes to your company's mix of products or services. In finance, if you have two portfolios offering a 20% return, you choose the less risky one, because it will create more value over time. The same is true with product portfolios.

Companies looking to recalibrate their product or service mix have essentially three options:

Focus narrowly

In October 2010 *Bloomberg Businessweek* ran a cover story with the sensationalist title "What Amazon Fears Most." The article profiled Quidsi, a relatively small New Jersey–based internet start-up cofounded by Marc Lore (a former student of ours) and best known for its main venture, the online retailer Diapers.com.

Diapers would appear to be a terrible product to sell on the internet. They are bulky and expensive to ship, and they have low margins because *everyone*—from convenience stores to Costco— sells them. But diapers have one thing going for them: Demand is highly predictable—birthrates are stable, and infants pee and poop constantly over an extended period of time. Also, product variety is limited, because there are only three or four major diaper manufacturers, and diapers come in just a few sizes. Given that every newly acquired customer will use the product repeatedly for two years or more, the company can count on a steady revenue stream with little or no risk for a long time to come.

Focused business models are most effective when they appeal to distinct market segments with clearly differentiated needs. So if your business currently serves multiple segments, it may be best to subdivide into focused units rather than try to apply one model. Amazon, which bought both Quidsi and the online shoe and apparel retailer Zappos, allows its focused acquisitions considerable autonomy in serving their segments.

Idea in Brief

The Problem

Business model innovation is typically an ad hoc process, lacking any framework for exploring opportunities. As a result, many companies miss out on inexpensive ways to radically improve their profitability and productivity.

The Solution

Drawing on the idea that a business model reflects a set of decisions, the authors frame innovation in terms of deciding what products or services to offer, when to make decisions, who should make them, and why the decision makers choose as they do.

An Example

Traditional call centers hire a staff to supply services as needed from a place of work, incurring significant up-front costs and risks. LiveOps created a new model by revising the order of decisions: It employs agents as calls come in by routing the calls to home-based freelancers who have signaled their availability.

The main drawback for a focused business is that it must rely on a single product, service, or customer segment—and it may omit key customer needs. People buy both bread *and* butter.

Search for commonalities across products

The success of Volkswagen owes much to a strategy whereby its cars share components. Although the strategy does not protect VW from general demand swings, it reduces demand variability for individual components, because shared components make it easy for VW to switch production at its plants from one model to another whenever the demand for car models shifts.

Commonalities aren't just shared components among different products. They may also be the capabilities needed to serve various product, customer, and market segments. Consequently, companies can add to their mix products or services that reflect new applications of their capabilities. For instance, in the late 1990s Amazon expanded from books into music, video, and games—all of which required the same logistics capabilities that books did. This allowed the company to cover the risk of failing to acquire enough share in any one of these categories with a potentially superior share in another.

Commonality can, however, carry significant costs if components must be engineered for a wide range of makes and models. What's more, the strategy requires that the component-sharing products not all experience their demand highs and lows simultaneously.

Create a hedged portfolio

Just as financial institutions try to create portfolios of investments that will hedge one another's risks, companies can select an assortment of products or markets to reduce the overall riskiness of the business model. Chile's LAN Airlines takes such an approach: Unlike most major U.S. carriers, which derive less than 5% of their revenue from cargo, LAN uses the same wide-body planes, flying international routes, to transport both passengers and cargo.

Because almost all travel from the Americas to Europe is on overnight flights, passenger-only airlines keep their planes on the ground for long periods. LAN uses the downtime to carry cargo: A plane to Santiago that has picked up cargo in Europe can deliver it to other Chilean cities before returning to Santiago for its next overnight flight.

This approach reduces the risks associated with LAN's capacity decisions. Airlines make such decisions infrequently—by ordering new airplanes—and they are hard to reverse, leaving the companies vulnerable to periods of over- or underutilized capacity, with harsh effects on revenue. Hedging passengers with cargo mitigates this risk because their respective demand curves rarely rise or fall in concert. Moreover, carrying cargo allows the airline to fly profitably with fewer passengers, so it can afford to serve destinations that other airlines avoid.

Clearly, the approach works mainly for product and market combinations in which demand fluctuations are negatively correlated. For example, a manufacturer of ski apparel could hedge sales in North America with sales in South America—where the seasons are opposite. Overall demand stays fairly constant.

When Should You Make Your Key Decisions?

Decisions must often be made before you have enough information to make them with confidence. We have identified three strategies that, depending on the circumstances, can improve a business model by changing the timing of decisions.

Postpone the decision

In many industries companies make firm decisions about prices well before they actually sell anything. This, of course, often exposes them to risk. It's risky to price airplane seats early, for instance, because demand on any given route is highly contingent on economic and other conditions and can vary by the time of day, the day of the week, or the week of the month.

American Airlines solved this problem in the 1980s by using the booking system known as SABRE (for semi-automated business research environment), which makes it relatively easy to alter prices quickly by factoring in new information. The ability to price dynamically changed the airline industry forever. On any given flight, the price that passengers have actually paid to fly—even within the same seating class—can vary tremendously. Recently Uber, a company that matches customers who need rides with vehicles for hire, borrowed the same toolbox: In high-demand periods, the company implements "surge pricing," whereby prices for rides go up, reducing demand while increasing supply.

Price quotes can be delayed at the individual level. The casino and hospitality company Caesars Entertainment uses a sophisticated database compiled by its Total Rewards loyalty program. When a repeat customer calls to make a reservation, the agent asks for his Total Rewards number, which links to detailed information about the customer's gambling habits (including average bet size) and hence the profit he is likely to bring the casino. Depending on what the agent sees, the customer may hear anything from "Sorry, all our rooms are booked" to "You're in luck! We can offer you a complimentary stay in our Presidential Suite!"

Change the order of your decisions

Some companies don't have the option of changing the time frame within which they operate, but they *can* shuffle the order in which decisions are made in order to delay investment commitments until pertinent information is known.

Most product development, for example, begins with proposing a solution or a technology for a customer need. If, after initial investments, the solution proves to be a dud, then it's back to the drawing board. But an increasing number of companies, including the open-innovation pioneers InnoCentive and Hypios, have figured out that if they switch that sequence to *performance first, investment after,* they can shift much of the risk of R&D onto others.

These companies offer clients ("seekers") a secure website on which to present R&D problems to a global freelance community of qualified engineers, product designers, and scientists ("solvers"). The companies help seekers define their problems—which might range from the chemical synthesis of a specific molecule to designing the look and feel of a new product—with enough specificity to interest an appropriately skilled subset of solvers. Seekers offer monetary rewards for the right solutions (sometimes more than one is selected), and solvers compete to develop the best solutions and win the rewards.

A similar change in sequence explains the success of one company in the call center industry: LiveOps. Traditional centers make up-front investments in facilities and hard infrastructure (primarily communications) before they sign a single client or take their first call. They must also decide how many agents to hire, at what levels of skill and expertise, and provide training. Next they must sign up clients whose needs match the capabilities they have assembled. Finally, they must develop daily and weekly staffing plans to ensure that enough agents with the right skills will be available to handle calls.

LiveOps, in contrast, employs agents as the calls come in. Its agents work independently from home and signal LiveOps when they are ready to take calls. They are paid according to the duration of a call and—because calls are automatically recorded and scored—their skill at meeting callers' needs. Intelligent software routes callers to the most qualified agents available according to the nature of the call, so capacity and staffing are constantly adjusted *in real time* to meet actual demand.

This approach has its limits. Training on-demand employees in advance is difficult, and because they assume the risk of being idle and making no money, the business model depends on having an ample supply of people for whom downtime has a relatively low cost.

Split up the key decisions

The lean startup movement is taking the corporate innovation and start-up worlds by storm (see "Why the Lean Start-Up Changes Everything," later in this volume). At the heart of the movement is a new approach for entrepreneurs who are making decisions about their businesses. In the past, starting a risky new venture involved putting together a detailed business plan that would cover all essential pieces of the business model and then executing on the plan. All the key decisions were made at once and up front.

The lean start-up approach divides up the key decisions. A venture starts with relatively imprecise and limited hypotheses about where an opportunity may lie. Multiple stages of information gathering and "pivoting" follow, as the business model is revised to arrive at the final, validated version. Typically, the founders radically change their hypotheses as the venture unfolds.

In the start-up world, this approach is today the rule rather than the exception. BBureau, a mobile beauty and wellness service that was born in our classroom (one of us is an investor and board member), is a case in point. Rather than commit up front to one target market and a fixed portfolio of services, BBureau ran a number of small experiments on many different markets to identify the combinations of customers and services that would be most lucrative for its pop-up delivery model, effectively splitting the venture-design decision into a number of smaller ones.

After numerous rounds of experimentation and refinement, the team converged on a business model that included offering wellness services (such as massages) at boutique hotels and frequently repeated beauty services (such as nail treatments) at office locations. Those combinations kept the company's delivery costs low while ensuring a high customer willingness to pay.

This approach depends on finding decisions that can be divided up. In some cases the decision process is indivisible. (You can't price a little bit now and a little bit later.) In other cases it can be divided up only at some additional cost, and risk-return calculations should be performed.

Who Are the Best Decision Makers?

Many companies find that they can radically improve decision making in the value chain simply by changing the people who make the calls. Companies can:

Appoint a better-informed decision maker

The whole employee empowerment movement is based on giving decision rights to the most informed person or organization. Google's engineers, for example, have extraordinary freedom to decide what development projects the company should pursue, because Google believes they are better informed about technologies and tastes than the company's executives are.

The best-informed people aren't always in the company. More than 25 years ago, Walmart transferred some decision rights about stocking its store shelves to Procter & Gamble, because it saw that a supplier had the right combination of information and incentives to keep Walmart well stocked with products by optimizing delivery and production schedules. This has become a standard arrangement with the company's large suppliers.

More recently, we've seen decisions being made by algorithms. In the restaurant business, for example, servers are often scheduled for shifts they would rather not work and not scheduled for those they want. Worse, the least-productive servers are frequently put on the most-profitable shifts.

To get around this problem, the Boston-based restaurant chain Not Your Average Joe's uses an analytic tool called Muse, which was developed by Objective Logistics, a start-up in Cambridge, Massachusetts (in which one of us is both an adviser and an investor). Muse tracks servers' performance over time according to sales per customer (as measured by check size) and customer satisfaction (as measured by tips or directly). This has enabled the chain to develop a productivity-based ranking system whereby servers can schedule themselves, choosing both their shifts and the tables they serve.

Although the advantages of making decisions using better information are obvious, empowering employees, suppliers, or customers and collecting extensive data often entail costs and difficulties. Walmart made a considerable up-front investment in the largest private satellite network in the world in order to enable seamless data flow, and the company had to negotiate and coordinate complicated new relationships with trading partners.

Pass the decision risk to the party that can best manage the consequences

The key to Amazon's early prosperity was its drop-shipping model, which allowed it to offer more than a million books while stocking only 2,000 or so of the most popular titles. For the rest, Amazon forwarded orders to book wholesalers or publishers, who then often shipped the products directly to customers using Amazon packaging.

In this innovative model, Amazon's network of wholesalers and publishers independently managed their inventories. They, not Amazon, bore the risk of carrying books without knowing the likely demand for them. But because the risk was widely distributed, all were able to manage their own bits of it with relative ease.

Shifting the decision risk to the party best able to bear it is often an attractive strategy when no decision maker clearly has superior information. In its early years, Amazon was too small and too cash constrained to stock every single book in its catalog, whereas bigger wholesalers were well positioned to match supply with demand from Amazon and thousands of other small retailers. But for this strategy to work, the replacement decision maker's incentives must

Amazon's Path

FOUNDED IN 1994 with the U.S. book market in mind, Amazon has adopted many of the strategies in our framework over the years.

1996

Pass the decision risk to the party that can best manage the consequences
Cash-strapped, the company gets distributors and publishers to carry slow-moving inventory, rather than stocking the books itself.

1997

Integrate the incentives
Partners can't keep up with Amazon's growth and quick shipping promise, so the company reverses course and builds its own warehouses.

1998

Search for commonalities across products
Success with books leads to expansion into music, video, and games—where the company's logistics competencies can be applied.

2001

Pass the decision risk to the party that can best manage the consequences
Amazon hosts the websites of Toys "R" Us, Borders, and Target and performs most site development, order fulfillment, and customer service.

2005

Change the revenue stream
Per-item shipping costs deter many customers, so Amazon offers Amazon Prime: Customers buy a shipping subscription rather than paying for individual shipments. This also encourages impulse purchases.

Postpone the decision
The acquisition of BookSurge (on-demand book publishing) and CreateSpace (self-publishing of books, CDs, DVDs, and video) allows Amazon to delay publication decisions until customer tastes are known.

2006

Appoint a better-informed decision maker
Amazon takes over retailers' A-to-Z fulfillment function—a logical extension of its third-party services.

Create a hedged portfolio
Amazon expands into computing services including storage, simple queue service (SQS), cloud computing, and electronic data systems.

2008–2010

Focus narrowly
Amazon realizes efficiencies by acquiring focused verticals: Diapers.com (baby consumables) and Zappos (shoes). Acquired retailers operate independently to maintain these efficiencies.

---

be aligned with yours. Amazon's model would have failed if the publishers had been motivated to poach its customers.

Select the decision maker with the most to gain
In many business models, key decisions are made by those with less to gain than others in the chain. A company's customers, for example, often feel that they gain less when they buy a company's products than the company does. That was a problem facing Netafim, the Israeli market leader in drip-irrigation technology.

Drip irrigation is the watering method of choice for small farmers in hot countries. Netafim developed a technology that fine-tunes water application according to the soil's water content, salinity, and fertilization and to meteorological data. The company demonstrated to farmers that its system could increase crop yields by 300% to 500%, making it a potentially lucrative investment.

Initially, though, the technology was a hard sell. Small farmers were reluctant to engage with and pay for anything so sophisticated. They did not trust the company and felt that they were shouldering a lot of risk in adopting its approach. Netafim solved the problem by offering them a free integrated package that included system design and installation, all required hardware, and periodic maintenance. Payback came from a share of each farmer's increased crop yields. Thus Netafim took on all the risks of the decision, and farmers simply said yes or no to a strong chance of earning more money with no downside.

Netafim could do this because it realized that it had the most to gain from the adoption of its technology. Given its expertise and access to sophisticated forecasting systems, the risks were a lot smaller for the company than for the individual farmers. Moreover, it could spread the risk: If the system failed at one farm, Netafim could make up for it elsewhere. As farmers achieved greater success, word would spread; Netafim would increase its sales and realize economies of scale.

Something similar is at work with energy-efficiency companies, many of which essentially take on energy management for their customers, implementing whatever efficiencies they think necessary and bearing all the up-front costs. They then share the savings that result from these improvements with the customers. Like Netafim, they bear additional risk quite easily, because they understand the technology and can predict its performance. And as resistance to adoption declines, their revenues scale up.

There are catches. A company can safely take on more risk only if the relevant technology is very reliable. And behavioral issues may arise: The savings from energy-efficient equipment will shrink if customers decide that they can economically leave their lights on longer.

Why Do Key Decision Makers Choose as They Do?

When decision makers collaborate to create value, they must also be able to pursue their private objectives without damaging the value chain. Many business model innovations, therefore, come from adjusting decision makers' motivations. There are three ways of doing this:

Change the revenue stream

Traditionally, when the U.S. Department of Defense bought aircraft, it would agree to a time-and-materials contract, under which suppliers charged for labor and materials consumed (on a cost-plus basis) in the course of each maintenance event—just as a mechanic does for car repairs. Unfortunately, this model doesn't provide suppliers with customer-friendly incentives; from their point of view, the more problems the client has, the better. It has been estimated that for every dollar the government spent to buy a new airplane, it spent seven more over the plane's life.

Until, that is, the DoD gave suppliers a reason to care about engine reliability. In 2003, facing pressure to cut costs and improve performance, the department adopted what's called performance-based contracting, which changed the revenue model for contractors. They would be paid for the amount of time the aircraft was actually in service, with the DoD specifying, for example, 95% availability as its threshold. As a result, the longer a jet performed without needing to be taken out of service for maintenance or repair, the more the contractor earned.

Changing the revenue stream to align the interests of a decision's stakeholders works best when performance can be fully and unambiguously defined. It would be difficult to set reasonable performance standards and develop appropriate metrics for, say, a new airplane that relied on advanced technologies and materials, because the unknowns involved would simply be too numerous.

Synchronize the time horizons

Traditionally, sourcing relied on competitive-bidding rituals that ensured low prices and moderate but acceptable quality. The chosen provider won the business for a relatively short period of time, after which the bidding process was repeated.

But as overseas sourcing increased, this model developed flaws. Faraway suppliers cut corners on quality control and materials reliability. Worse, revelations of abusive labor practices, product diversion, and the counterfeiting of goods emerged. And because most sourcing transactions were one-off deals, shoddy providers faced few consequences—until, of course, multinationals felt the corrosive impact of repeated performance problems on their brands.

Enter Li & Fung, a Hong Kong–based company that has changed the world of outsourcing by creating a new business model based on combining the flexibility of competitive sourcing with the confidence of long-term relationships. It selects, verifies, and approves suppliers and allocates their business among its manufacturing clients, and it manages each client's relationship with each supplier—including performance, compliance, and crafting incentives for suppliers to invest in people, facilities, and materials. Given the potential for an enduring relationship with Li & Fung, suppliers are motivated to create long-term value for manufacturing partners.

But companies like Li & Fung are few and far between. If your organization sources in sectors or regions where you lack recourse to a trusted intermediary, you will need to manage such relationships directly, which can be difficult.

Integrate the incentives

Companies without a trusted intermediary can develop contractual arrangements and management systems (such as the famous balanced scorecard) to focus independent agents on maximizing an agreed-upon outcome. This is essentially what one of the most promising reforms to U.S. health care is about: Under the bundled payments system, all parties involved in a patient's treatment agree to measure performance according to the outcome for the patient (see "How to Design a Bundled Payment Around Value," on hbr.org).

Sometimes such contractual arrangements can be so complex that it's easier to simply integrate operations. Quad/Graphics, a printing company with approximately 25,000 employees and annual revenue of more than $4 billion, has created its own health care system, complete with doctors and hospitals, lowering health care costs for its employees by some 30% in the process. Patient outcomes have improved as well: For example, the rate of cesarean-section births among women in the Quad health care system is only 12%, compared with 26% nationally.

Achieving full integration is not trivial; many organizations rightly hesitate to take on directly performing activities that are outside their core competencies. Thus we tend to regard it as a last resort, to be applied only when other approaches won't suffice.

Using a framework like ours, any experienced manager can find ways to create a better business model. Companies can also use the framework to make their innovation processes more systematic and open, with business model reinvention becoming a continual, inclusive process rather than a series of isolated, internally focused events. When they do, they find that the resulting capabilities offer a sustainable competitive advantage.

Originally published in July–August 2014. Reprint R1407H

The Transformative Business Model

by Stelios Kavadias, Kostas Ladas, and Christoph Loch

WE USUALLY ASSOCIATE an industry's transformation with the adoption of a new technology. But although new technologies are often major factors, they have never transformed an industry on their own. What does achieve such a tranformation is a business model that can link a new technology to an emerging market need.

MP3 technology is a classic case in point. Early MP3 devices represented an order-of-magnitude increase in capacity over magnetic tapes and CDs: Users could carry thousands of songs on a small device. But MP3 players revolutionized the audio devices market only after Apple coupled the iPod with iTunes in a new business model, swiftly moving music-recording sales from the physical to the virtual world.

What, exactly, enables a business model to deliver on a technology's potential? To answer that question, we embarked on an in-depth analysis of 40 companies that had launched new business models in a variety of industries. Some succeeded in radically altering their industries; others looked promising but ultimately did not succeed. In this article we present the key takeaways from our research and suggest how they can help innovators transform industries.

How Business Models Work

Definitions of "business model" vary, but most people would agree that it describes how a company creates and captures value. The features of the model define the customer value proposition and the pricing mechanism, indicate how the company will organize itself and whom it will partner with to produce value, and specify how it will structure its supply chain. Basically, a business model is a system whose various features interact, often in complex ways, to determine the company's success.

In any given industry, a dominant business model tends to emerge over time. In the absence of market distortions, the model will reflect the most efficient way to allocate and organize resources. Most attempts to introduce a new model fail—but occasionally one succeeds in overturning the dominant model, usually by leveraging a new technology. If new entrants use the model to displace incumbents, or if competitors adopt it, then the industry has been transformed.

Consider Airbnb, which upended the hotel industry. Founded in 2008, the company has experienced phenomenal growth: It now has more rooms than either InterContinental Hotels or Hilton Worldwide. As of this writing, Airbnb represents 19.5% of the hotel room supply in New York and operates in 192 countries, in which it accounts for 5.4% of room supply (up from 3.6% in 2015).

The founders of Airbnb realized that platform technology made it feasible to craft an entirely new business model that would challenge the traditional economics of the hotel business. Unlike conventional hotel chains, Airbnb does not own or manage property—it allows users to rent any livable space (from a sofa to a mansion) through an online platform that matches individuals looking for accommodations with home owners willing to share a room or a house. Airbnb manages the platform and takes a percentage of the rent.

Because its income does not depend on owning or managing physical assets, Airbnb needs no large investments to scale up and thus can charge lower prices (usually 30% lower than hotels charge). Moreover, since the home owners are responsible for managing and maintaining the property and any services they may offer, Airbnb's risks (not to mention operational costs) are much lower than those of traditional hotels. On the customer side, Airbnb's model redefines the value proposition by offering a more personal service—and a cheaper one.

Before platform technology existed, there was no reason to change the hotel business in any meaningful way. But after its

Idea in Brief

The Question

No new technology can transform an industry unless a business model can link it to an emerging market need. How can you tell whether a model will succeed in doing that?

The Research

The authors undertook an in-depth analysis of 40 companies that launched new business models in a variety of industries. Some had transformed their industries; others looked promising but ultimately didn't succeed.

The Findings

Transformative business models tend to include three or more of these features: (1) personalization, (2) a closed-loop process, (3) asset sharing, (4) usage-based pricing, (5) a collaborative ecosystem, and (6) an agile and adaptive organization.

introduction, the dominant business model became vulnerable to attack from anyone who could leverage that technology to create a more compelling value proposition for customers. The new business model serves as the interface between *what technology enables* and *what the marketplace wants*.

Let's look now at what features make a business model transformative.

The Six Keys to Success

We selected the 40 new business models we analyzed on the basis of how many mentions they received in the high-quality, high-circulation business press. All of them seemed to have the *potential* to transform their industries, but only a subset had succeeded in doing so. We looked for recurring features in the models and found six. No company displayed all of them, but as we shall see, a higher number of these features usually correlated with a higher chance of success at transformation.

1. **A more personalized product or service.** Many new models offer products or services that are better tailored than the dominant models to customers' individual and immediate needs. Companies often leverage technology to achieve this at competitive prices.

2. **A closed-loop process.** Many models replace a linear consumption process (in which products are made, used, and then disposed of) with a closed loop, in which used products are recycled. This shift reduces overall resource costs.

3. **Asset sharing.** Some innovations succeed because they enable the sharing of costly assets—Airbnb allows home owners to share them with travelers, and Uber shares assets with car owners. Sometimes assets may be shared across a supply chain. The sharing typically happens by means of two-sided online marketplaces that unlock value for both sides: I get money from renting my spare room, and you get a cheaper and perhaps nicer place to stay. Sharing also reduces entry barriers to many industries, because an entrant need not own the assets in question; it can merely act as an intermediary.

4. **Usage-based pricing.** Some models charge customers when they use the product or service, rather than requiring them to buy something outright. The customers benefit because they incur costs only as offerings generate value; the company benefits because the number of customers is likely to grow.

5. **A more collaborative ecosystem.** Some innovations are successful because a new technology improves collaboration with supply chain partners and helps allocate business risks more appropriately, making cost reductions possible.

6. **An agile and adaptive organization.** Innovators sometimes use technology to move away from traditional hierarchical models of decision making in order to make decisions that better reflect market needs and allow real-time adaptation to changes in those needs. The result is often greater value for the customer at less cost to the company.

Each feature on this list is tied to long-term trends in both technology and demand. (See the exhibit "Linking technology and the market.") On the tech side, one trend is the development of sensors that allow cheaper and broader data capture. Another is that big data, artificial intelligence, and machine learning are enabling

Linking technology and the market

The six features that characterize successful innovation all link a recognized technology trend and a recognized market need. Trends were identified by an analysis of regularly published industry reports from think tanks and consulting companies such as the McKinsey Global Institute, PwC, and the Economist Intelligence Unit.

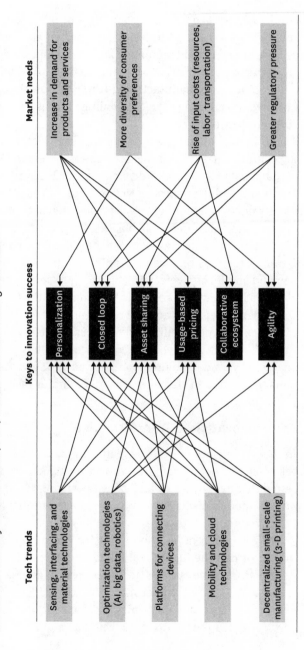

companies to turn enormous amounts of unstructured data into rules and decisions. A third is that connected devices (the internet of things) and cloud technology are permitting decentralized and widespread data manipulation and analysis. And a fourth is that developments in manufacturing (think nanotechnology and 3-D printing) are creating more possibilities for distributed and small-scale production.

On the market side, although the steady progress of developing countries has led to a stable increase in demand worldwide, it is complicated by a greater diversity in customer preferences (both across and within countries). Higher factor prices (despite the commodity price reductions of 2015) and heightened regulation (notably on environmental effects and business conduct) further increase the challenges for companies looking to gain market share.

All six features represent potential solutions for linking market demand and technological capability. For example, greater personalization in the value proposition responds to the fragmentation of consumer preferences and the resultant demand for more-diverse offerings. That personalization has been made possible by sensors that collect data from connected devices via the cloud; the data is analyzed by big data solutions and turned into services—such as recommendations and alerts—that are different for each user.

From Innovation to Transformation

In theory, the more of the six features a new business model has, the greater its potential to transform a given industry should be. We tested that hypothesis by analyzing how many features each of the 40 new models displayed and comparing the results with its actual performance.

We gave each model one point for each feature on which it outperformed the incumbent business model. We then assessed its transformative success according to the degree to which the model had attracted market share (displacing incumbents) and the extent to which other companies had copied it. Our results strongly suggest (that's the best one can get from statistical analyses) that business models with transformative potential tend to have three or more of the six features. (See the exhibit "How many boxes should a model tick?")

The taxi service company Uber ticks no fewer than five boxes. Its business model is built on asset sharing—the drivers use their own cars. Uber has developed a *collaborative ecosystem* in which the driver assumes the risk of winning rides, while the platform helps minimize that risk through the application of big data. The platform also creates *agility* through an internal decision-making system that responds to market changes in real time. This lets Uber apply *usage-based pricing* and direct drivers to locations where the probability of finding a fare is high.

Finally, Uber uses a scheme whereby customers rate drivers. Via the big data platform, a would-be customer can see on his or her mobile device the closest drivers and their ratings. The rating system pushes drivers to offer clean cars and quality service, and it also provides at least a bit of *personalization*. Allowing the customer to decide between the closest car and the one (maybe a bit farther out) with the highest rating may not sound like much, but it is still far ahead of traditional taxi services.

The implication of our finding is straightforward: If you are thinking about changing your business model or entering an industry with a new model, you can rate yourself on how well your model performs on the six features. If you don't beat the competition on any of them, your chances of success are low. But if your model significantly outdoes the current model on three or more features, you are well positioned to succeed.

To rate yourself on a feature, you must first define what it actually means in your industry. For example, in financial services *personalization* may mean tailored loan terms (including interest rates, monthly payments, and loan duration), whereas in retail it may mean customized T-shirt designs or one-off dresses. In education it may mean that the support provided to students changes according to their individual strengths and weaknesses, and in health care it may mean data-enabled, targeted medicine. Only when performance is expressed in such industry-specific ways can a company develop

Our research suggests that to transform an industry, a business model must display at least three of the six key features. Here's how the 40 new models we examined stacked up.

	Business	Industry	Personalization	Closed loop	Asset sharing	Usage-based pricing	Collaborative ecosystem	Agility	Score
1	Airbnb	Real estate	X		X		X	X	4
2	Alibaba	Retail	X			X	X		3
3	Amazon	Retail	X			X	X	X	4
4	Appear Here	Real estate rentals			X		X		2
5	Apple iPod	Electronics	X			X	X		3
6	Arm	Electronics	X			X	X	X	3
7	Canon	Electronics/copiers		X			X		3
8	Coursera	Education	X			X	X		2
9	Dell	Electronics	X			X	X	X	4
10	Edx	Education	X				X		2
11	Etsy	Retail	X						1
12	Google Adwords	Advertising	X			X	X	X	4
13	Handy	Home services				X	X		2

	Business	Industry	Personalization	Closed loop	Asset sharing	Usage-based pricing	Collaborative ecosystem	Agility	Score
14	IKEA	Retail	X	X			X	X	4
15	Interface	Carpeting		X		X			2
16	JustPark	Real estate	X		X	X	X		3
17	LEGO Factory	Toys	X			X	X	X	4
18	Lending Club	Banking				X		X	2
19	Liveops	Call centers			X		X	X	3
20	Lyft	Taxi operation	X		X	X	X		4
21	M-Pesa	Banking	X		X		X		3
22	Medicast	Health care	X		X		X		3
23	Natura	Cosmetics		X			X		2
24	Nike ID	Footwear	X					X	2
25	Philips pay per lux	Lighting		X	X	X	X		4
26	Ricoh pay per page	Electronics		X		X	X		3
27	Rolls-Royce power-by-the-hour	Engines		X		X	X	X	4
28	Ryanair	Transportation				X	X	X	3
29	Salesforce.com	Software	X		X	X	X		3

(continued)

How many boxes should a model tick? (Continued)

	Business	Industry	Personalization	Closed loop	Asset sharing	Usage-based pricing	Collaborative ecosystem	Agility Score
30	Shyp	Transport & logistics	X	X			X	3
31	TaskRabbit	Home services			X	X		2
32	Tencent QQ	Software	X			X	X	3
33	Uber	Taxi operation	X		X	X	X	5
34	Udacity	Education	X				X	2
35	Washio	Dry cleaning	X		X	X		3
36	Wayfair	Home goods		X			X	3
37	Xerox	Electronics				X	X	2
38	Zara	Apparel	X				X	3
39	Zipcar	Transportation	X		X	X	X	4
40	Zopa	Banking	X		X	X	X	4

metrics to evaluate and compare its model on the key features and begin to think about how to differentiate itself by using new technologies.

Healx: A Case Study

Informed by our business model framework, we advised (and Cambridge Judge Business School's business accelerator supported) the tech venture Healx, which focuses on the treatment of patients with rare diseases in the emerging field of personalized medicine. A big challenge for pharmaceutical companies in this domain is that rare-disease markets are very small, so companies usually have to charge astronomical prices. (One drug, Soliris, used in the treatment of paroxysmal nocturnal hemoglobinuria, costs about $500,000 per patient-year.) Some potential treatments are, however, being used for more-common diseases with large patient markets. They could be repurposed to suit the needs of rare-disease sufferers, but they typically work only for people with specific genetic profiles.

Enter Healx, with a platform that leverages big data technology and analytics across multiple databases owned by various organizations within global life sciences and health care to efficiently match treatments to rare-disease patients. Its initial business model hit three of our six key features. First, Healx's value proposition was about *asset sharing* (for example, making available clinical-trial databases that record the effectiveness of most drugs across therapeutic areas and diseases, including rare ones). Second, the business promised more *personalization* by revealing drugs with high potential for treating the rare diseases covered. Finally, Healx's model would, in theory, create a *collaborative ecosystem* by bringing together big pharma (which has the treatment and trial data) and health care providers (which have data about effectiveness and incompatibility reactions and also personal genome descriptions).

How did we measure performance along those features? To assess *personalization,* we compared the amount of drug data currently provided to sufferers of rare diseases with the amount that Healx could provide, which initially covered 1,000 of the 7,000 rare diseases that have formal advocacy groups worldwide. These groups represent some 350 million people, 95% of whom currently get no even reasonably relevant drug recommendations. We measured *asset sharing* by looking at the proportion of known data on rare-disease-relevant drugs that Healx could access—about 20% in its start-up phase. Finally, we assessed its *collaborative ecosystem* by looking at how many of the main data-holding institutions participated—about a quarter.

At first Healx struggled to get pharma companies to join the platform; they were concerned that their treatment data would leak to competitors. But the Healx team spotted an opportunity to give companies an incentive. In 2014 the United Kingdom's National Health Service introduced a new rule for pharmaceutical companies: If an expensive treatment doesn't work for a patient, the company responsible can be forced to reimburse NHS providers for its cost. The reimbursement amounts were disease-specific and counted in the thousands of British pounds.

Treatment failure is often caused by specificities in individual genomes, and Healx's managers realized that their technology could help companies predict such failures with high accuracy, potentially saving millions of pounds a year.

More recently, Healx has developed a machine-learning algorithm that can use a patient's biological information not only to match drugs to disease symptoms but also to predict exactly which drug will achieve what level of effectiveness for that particular patient. The latest version of its business model brings *personalization* to the maximum possible level and adds *agility,* because the treating clinician—armed with the biological data and the algorithm—can make better treatment decisions directly with the patient and doesn't have to rely on fixed rules of thumb about which of the few available off-label drugs to use. In this way, Healx is able to support decentralized, real-time, accurate decision making.

This version of the Healx model has even more transformation potential—it exhibits four of the six features; it has already generated revenue from customers; and in the long term it could empower patients by giving them much more information before they consult a medical practitioner. Although it is still too early to tell whether that potential will be realized, Healx is clearly a venture to watch. It has earned a number of prizes (including the 2015 Life Science Business of the Year and the 2016 Graduate Business of the Year in the Cambridge cluster) and sizable investments from several global funds.

You cannot guarantee the success of an innovation (unless you choose a market niche so small as to be insignificant). But you can load the dice by ensuring that your business model links market needs with emerging technologies. The more such links you can make, the more likely you are to transform your industry.

Originally published in October 2016. Reprint R1610H

Competing Against Free

by David J. Bryce, Jeffrey H. Dyer, and Nile W. Hatch

A NEW COMPETITOR ENTERS YOUR market and offers a product very similar to yours but with one key difference: It's free. Do you ignore it, hoping that your customers won't defect or the free product won't last? Or do you rapidly introduce a free product of your own in an attempt to quash the threat? These are questions faced by an increasing number of companies—and not just in the digital realm. The "free" business models popularized by companies such as Google, Adobe, and Mozilla are spreading to markets in the physical world, from pharmaceuticals to airlines to automobiles.

How should established companies respond? Clearly, managers are having difficulty figuring this out. For the past five years, we have been studying how incumbents have dealt with competitors employing free business models in a variety of product markets. (See the sidebar "About the Research.") We have found no examples of companies in the nondigital realm that have prevailed against rivals with free offerings. In fact, in two-thirds of the battles that have progressed far enough to be judged, incumbents (both digital and physical) made the wrong choice. In a handful of instances, companies that should not have taken action did so immediately by introducing their own free offering—hurting their revenues and profitability. They should have either waited and allowed the attacker to self-destruct or recognized that the two could peacefully coexist.

About the Research

FOR FIVE YEARS, we have been studying companies that face competition from rivals offering free products and services. The 34 incumbents we've been following are in 26 product markets representing the digital and physical realms as well as the intersection of the two. The markets include airlines, automobiles, classified advertising, dermatology pharmaceuticals, internet services, music, office applications, operating systems, personal finance software, radio, and telecommunications. Twenty-four of the battles between incumbents and free-product rivals have progressed far enough for us to judge the incumbents' actions. In two-thirds of those cases, the incumbents made the wrong choice: They introduced their own free offering too quickly, responded too slowly, or did nothing at all.

More commonly, companies that should have taken action didn't do so quickly enough or at all. Surprisingly, these included incumbents that had identified a genuine threat from a new entrant and had all the weapons they needed to win a head-to-head battle: an established customer base, superior product features, a strong reputation, and abundant financial resources.

Why didn't these companies use their formidable assets to fend off free-product competitors? The answer is so obvious that you've probably guessed it: Managers were reluctant to abandon an existing business model that was generating healthy revenues and profits. But if the answer is obvious, why did managers make this mistake? The reason is the ubiquity of the profit-center structure and mind-set. Drawing from our research on free offerings in online and physical markets, we explore in this article how to assess whether the introduction of a free product or service in your market is a threat and how to overcome the profit-center challenge.

Assessing the Threat

The seriousness of the threat posed by a new entrant hinges on three factors: the entrant's ability to cover its costs quickly enough, the rate at which the number of users of the free offering is growing, and the speed with which your paying customers are defecting.

Idea in Brief

Business models that involve offering a product or service for free and making money in other ways are spreading beyond the digital realm. But managers of threatened companies are having difficulty figuring out how to respond: An ongoing study has found that some companies respond too quickly but most don't do so quickly enough—even when they have sufficient resources.

To assess the threat, incumbents should consider the entrant's ability to cover its costs quickly enough, the rate at which the number of users of the free offering is growing, and the speed with which paying customers are defecting.

Three simple policies can make this new compact tangible. They are (1) hiring employees for explicit "tours of duty," (2) encouraging employees to build networks and expertise outside the organization, and (3) establishing active alumni networks to maintain career-long relationships.

Some new competitors self-destruct because they can't convert nonpaying customers into paying ones fast enough to cover costs or because they can't find a third party that will pay for access to their users. So it's crucial to determine if the competitor's free offering is generating revenue in some way. Of course, some companies may have enough funding to wait a year or more before they need to monetize their user base. (For example, Skype offered its free phone service for a year before it introduced SkypeOut, a paid service for calling landlines from a computer.) But this scenario can actually benefit an incumbent by giving it time to assess the potential of the model and decide whether to launch its own free product.

We learned that an entrant will usually find a way to turn users into revenue-generating customers if its user base is growing rapidly or if the incumbent's paying customers are defecting to the free offering at a high rate. What rates signal danger? Our examination of the dynamics in a number of markets suggests that if the free offering's user base is growing by 40% or more a year (meaning that it will at least double every two years) or your customer defection rate is 5% or more a year (meaning that you stand to lose at least 25% of your customers within five years), serious trouble may be looming. As the exhibit "How big a threat is 'free' competition?"

How big a threat is "free" competition?

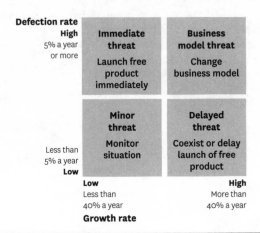

	Low	High
Defection rate **High** 5% a year or more	**Immediate threat** Launch free product immediately	**Business model threat** Change business model
Less than 5% a year **Low**	**Minor threat** Monitor situation	**Delayed threat** Coexist or delay launch of free product
	Low Less than 40% a year	**High** More than 40% a year
	Growth rate	

shows, assessing those rates (or reasonable estimates of them) helps a company determine the level of threat from the free product and respond accordingly.

Choosing Whether and When to Respond

When both rates mentioned above are high, the entrant represents a *business model* threat. Most established companies must not only respond with a free offering but also radically change their business model to survive. And they need to do so pretty quickly—within two or three years. Many newspapers competing against online rivals that offer free classified advertising or editorial content are in this quadrant. They will continue to deteriorate sharply without a fundamental rethinking of their business model.

Fortunately for incumbents, most threats wind up in one of the other quadrants, which means there may be more time to respond. When the entrant's users are multiplying rapidly but the established firm's customers are defecting slowly, the entrant represents a *delayed* threat. This means the free product or service is attracting either customers from other established competitors or brand-new users. In such cases, your offering can coexist with the free one for at least a few years—especially if yours is targeting premium segments. This is the situation that Microsoft finds itself in with its Office software: Because of the high switching costs, most current enterprise users aren't defecting, but new users—college students, small businesses, and educational institutions—are increasingly using Google Docs and Oracle's Open Office, both of which are free. (See the sidebar "Why Microsoft Should Take Its 'Free' Competition More Seriously.")

The trick for incumbents facing delayed threats is figuring out exactly when to respond with either a free version of the existing offering or a new free product that appeals to new users. Responding sooner rather than later allows an incumbent to beat back the entrant and probably won't significantly hurt existing sales (because established customers are switching slowly). As soon as the entrant's users are in the millions, however, the incumbent must respond—as Intuit did when it acquired upstart Mint.com for $170 million in 2009, eliminating a threat to its Quicken personal finance software and gaining a free online product. (Mint.com had attracted more than 2 million users in just three years.)

When the defection rate among your paying customers is high and the growth rate of the entrant's users is low, the threat is obviously *immediate* because your revenues are rapidly eroding. Even though the free offering has not yet attracted a large following, it's a problem for you and demands a prompt response. It also suggests that you are overserving your customers and thereby inviting disruption. You must quickly figure out a way to launch a free offering.

Finally, when both rates are low, the threat is *minor*. In these cases, the incumbent should continue to monitor the situation.

Offer a Better Free

If you've established that free offerings are a threat to your business and have considered the timing of your response, the next step is to figure out *how* to respond. Most incumbents can successfully

Why Microsoft Should Take Its "Free" Competition More Seriously

FOR THE PAST FOUR YEARS, Microsoft's Office software has been under attack from free alternatives: Google Docs and Oracle's Open Office. Although Microsoft finally responded in 2010 with Microsoft Live, a free "cloud" version of Office, it waited too long and was not forceful enough to contain what could become a serious threat.

Microsoft's reluctance to embrace a free-product strategy is not surprising. Its office applications business has long enjoyed a near monopoly and has been highly profitable. And except for price-sensitive users such as college students and public entities, its customers have not flocked to the free products. Indeed, concerns about file incompatibility, the lack of functions in competing products, and the need to teach employees how to use new applications have kept the vast majority of Microsoft's target corporate customers in the fold.

But in our view, Microsoft has erred in not taking the defection among price-sensitive customers more seriously. Our survey of college students suggests that nearly 20% now exclusively use free alternatives, up from about 4% five years ago. According to a competitor, the number of students in the United States using Google Apps has increased from 7 million to 10 million in the past two years, and about 3 million small-business users and some large institutions (including Brown, the California State University system, Gonzaga, the University of Minnesota, the University of Virginia, Vanderbilt, Villanova, and William & Mary) have adopted it as well. This is a big problem for Microsoft: Open Office and Google Docs will continue to improve, becoming more attractive to younger and newer users as well as price-sensitive institutions—especially those overserved by the function-laden Office suite.

So far, Microsoft Live doesn't seem to be effective in countering the free offerings of its competitors. There are several possible reasons. One is that Microsoft, unlike Open Office, doesn't offer a version that can be downloaded to and operated from an individual computer. Another is that Microsoft has not promoted its free product aggressively enough, and, as a result, it is not as well-known as Google Docs.

Judging from Microsoft's half-hearted response to date, the company doesn't want customers switching to its free product. This is a mistake. By sacrificing a portion of revenues from price-sensitive or overserved customers, Microsoft could prevent free-product competitors from expanding their foothold and give itself a better shot at retaining its most valuable customers: the business and power home users who are loyal today but could ultimately defect.

counterattack by unleashing their arsenal of weapons, which typically includes a large base of users or customers who have made investments in learning how to use the product, advanced technical knowhow, substantial brand equity, significant financial resources, knowledge of the market, and access to important distribution and marketing channels. Incumbents can use those assets to introduce a better free product and to employ some tried-and-true sales and pricing strategies to generate revenues and profits: up-selling, cross-selling, selling access to customers, and bundling the free product with paid offerings. (See the sidebar "Four Tried-and-True Strategies.")

Yet, as we mentioned above, incumbents often fail to counterattack. A widely known case in point is the reluctance of almost all major newspapers in the United States to embrace a free business model when Craigslist attacked their profitable classified-ads business. According to our research, Salt Lake City is the only top 50 U.S. metropolitan market for classified ads that is not dominated by Craigslist. The reason? Deseret Media (which includes the *Deseret News*, KSL TV, and KSL NewsRadio) responded quickly to the business model threat by launching its own free classifieds site and making other significant changes. The site, ksl.com, is better developed and easier to navigate than Craigslist, and it leveraged the established KSL brand to attract classified ads.

Deseret Media quickly benefited from network effects: More buyers went to ksl.com than to Craigslist because more sellers were posting there. The site generates revenue by charging advertisers that want to post regular ads as well as classified sellers who want preferred positions. The site's profits now exceed those of the traditional businesses, including the newspaper.

Meanwhile, Deseret Media has changed the newspaper's business model by cutting nearly half its staff and crowdsourcing some of its content. In 2010, the paper increased its print and online audience by 15%, the second-highest growth rate in the industry. Overall, Deseret Media is thriving.

Yahoo is another example of an incumbent that prevailed by introducing a better free product. In 2004, Google launched its free

Four Tried-and-True Strategies

1. Up-sell

Introduce a free basic offering to gain widespread use and then charge for a premium version.

Requirements:

- A free product that appeals to a very large user base so that even a low conversion rate of users to paying customers will generate substantial revenues **or**
- A high percentage of users willing to pay for the premium version

Examples:

Virtually every iPhone app uses this strategy. One tactic is to offer a free version of the product to consumers and a premium version to the business market, as Adobe does with its Reader software.

Skype, which offers free computer-to-computer calls and charges for add-ons, succeeds with up-selling because it has more than 400 million users, many of whom become paying customers. Flickr, the free photo-sharing site, has a much smaller user base and a low conversion rate. That explains why eBay paid $2.6 billion for Skype, and Yahoo paid less than $30 million for Flickr.

2. Cross-sell

Sell other products that are not directly tied to the free product.

Requirements:

- A broad product line—preferably one that complements the free product—**or**
- The ability through partnerships to sell a broad line of products to users of the free product

Examples:

Ryanair offers roughly 25% of its airline seats free but cross-sells a variety of add-on services, such as seat reservations and priority boarding. Once on the plane, the customer is sold food, scratch-card games, perfume, digital cameras, MP3 players, and other products. (Ryanair employs a second strategy: charging third parties for in-flight advertisements.) Specialty pharmaceuticals company Galderma rebates out-of-pocket costs for Epiduo, a prescription acne gel, and cross-sells other skin care products.

3. Charge Third Parties

Provide a free product to users and then charge a third party for access to them.

Requirements:

- A free offering that attracts either many users who can be segmented for advertisers or a targeted group that makes up a customer segment **and**
- Third parties willing to pay to reach these users

Examples:

Google, which charges companies to advertise to its millions of users, is the poster child for this strategy. Another example is Finnish telecommunications company Blyk, which offers 200 free cell-phone minutes a month to 16-to-24-year-olds who fill out a survey and agree to receive ads. Blyk then sells access to and information about them. Blyk was recently acquired by Orange, the largest brand of France Telecom.

Generating users does not guarantee success. Xmarks offered web-browser add-on tools that attracted more than 2 million users—and plenty of venture capital. But the company recently shut down because it couldn't deliver a clear segment to advertisers.

4. Bundle

Offer a free product or service with a paid offering.

Requirements:

- Products or services that can be bundled with the free offering **or**
- A free product that needs regular maintenance or a complementary offering

Examples:

Here the "free" effect is largely psychological—the customer must buy the bundle to get the free product. Think of Hewlett-Packard, which often gives away a printer with the purchase of a computer.

Better Place plans to lease electric cars in Israel by bundling a free lease with a service contract. Customers would pay to swap out their battery packs.

Banks are increasingly bundling free services, such as accounts and stock trades, with paid services, such as investment accounts that require minimum balances. But the bundled product doesn't have to be related to the free one. Banks also give away iPods, iPads, and other products to customers opening accounts.

Companies That Prevailed

PERSONAL FINANCE software company **Intuit** responded to the threat from free rival Mint.com by purchasing the company. Mint.com, which makes money by selling access to its user base, lets Intuit maintain a free offering separate from its popular Quicken product.

Yahoo, the leading provider of free e-mail, responded to Google's entry by matching, and then exceeding, Gmail's free storage offer.

Gmail service, which provided 10 times more storage than Yahoo, the leading provider of free e-mail at the time. As a new entrant, Google could afford to offer significantly more storage because it had relatively few users. A Google executive told us, "We don't do something unless it is an order of magnitude better—maybe five to 10 times better—than what others are offering, particularly if we have to get users to switch from another free product to ours."

Google's entry created a dilemma for Yahoo, which generated some revenue from up-selling (persuading users to pay for more storage or other add-ons) but much more from advertisers (its real customers). To match Google's offer, Yahoo would have had to buy warehouses of servers to provide storage for its 125 million e-mail users—an investment that would have generated no additional revenues.

Yahoo decided to respond in a way that sent a message to Google and to its own e-mail users and advertisers: It immediately announced that it would match Google's offer of one gigabyte of free storage. A couple of years later, it began to offer unlimited storage. Those moves left Yahoo users with no reason to switch to Google—and left Google with few options for offering a better free product. Although the increased costs hurt Yahoo's profits in the short term, the company's share of the e-mail market continues to be several times larger than Google's. But Google has not given up: Gmail now serves as a platform for the company's other free products, such as Google Docs and Calendar. In the long run, this could make Gmail the better free product.

The most important lesson from these cases? If your user base is vital to your revenue stream, you must quickly offer a free product

Companies That Ignored the Threat

THE MAJOR AIRLINES IN EUROPE have been slow to respond to **Ryanair,** which offers free or deeply discounted tickets and charges for other services. Ryanair has made impressive gains in Europe; its share now exceeds that of Air France.

Satellite radio company **SiriusXM,** which offers subscription packages for its more than 180 channels, has done nothing to stem the loss of share to Pandora, which provides free radio over the internet and generates revenue by charging for ad-free service and selling access to its user base to third parties.

that is comparable or superior to the new competitor's. If you can, you should try to crush that competitor or at least prevent it from becoming powerful enough to mount a serious challenge.

Rethink Profit Centers

Two obstacles prevent managers at established companies from making the leap to free strategies. The first is the deeply rooted belief that products must generate a respectable level of revenues and profits on their own. The second is the profit-center structure and the accounting system it employs, which both reflect and reinforce this mind-set.

In stable competitive environments, profit centers are a godsend: They push P&L accountability down, usually to the product level; they place revenue and cost streams in the hands of an individual, clearly identifying where the buck stops; and they provide a career ladder for those hoping to oversee units with larger budgets. But profit centers have a dark side: They make it impossible for an organization to consider a product's revenues and costs separately—a perspective that's essential for conceiving and implementing a free-product strategy.

To fix this problem, profit responsibility must be pushed up to a management group that oversees revenue and cost streams from a much wider variety of sources than traditional profit centers do. Clearly, a company that relies primarily on free-product strategies, such as Google, will place this responsibility much higher in the organization than one that uses free offerings as a small part of a more comprehensive strategy.

In addition to moving profit responsibility higher, companies with free business models generally place responsibility for revenue streams and cost management at lower levels, and in separate hands. *Revenue managers* in these companies pursue all possible ways to increase revenues—except product price. Clearly, the job requires creativity, but revenue is typically generated in the four ways mentioned above: up-selling, cross-selling, selling access to users, and bundling.

A separate set of *product development managers* is responsible for overseeing costs and building in product features that will expand the user base as rapidly as possible. On the basis of conversations with current executives at Google, we estimate that only the CEO and three or four senior vice presidents have P&L responsibility there.

Clearly, tensions can arise between the revenue group and the product development group, and it pays to spell out how they will be resolved. For example, Google's product development group can nix revenue models it believes would damage the user experience. When the two groups can't resolve disagreements, the senior managers with P&L responsibility—and sometimes even the CEO— arbitrate.

Another culprit that undermines many companies' ability to offer free products is the cost accounting system, which is excellent for averaging costs across large numbers of products and then allocating overhead but not for identifying the *actual* cost of the last product or service sold. The distinction between average cost (what some call variable cost or total cost) and actual cost (what some call marginal cost) is important because the latter is almost always lower than the former, often dramatically so. Think of what it costs an airline to fly an empty seat on an otherwise full or mostly full airplane: essentially nothing. This principle applies in nearly every industry. Once an operation is up and running and costs are largely incurred, generating additional products or services adds very little to total costs. Company leaders can use this notion to their advantage as they consider alternative pricing approaches, such as free offerings. By stepping back from the cost accounting system, they may find flexibility they didn't realize they had.

An example from the pharmaceutical industry illustrates how the profit-center structure and mind-set and the cost accounting system make it difficult for established companies to react when rivals offer free products or services. In 2008, specialty pharmaceuticals manufacturer Galderma (a joint venture of Nestlé and L'Oréal) launched Epiduo, a prescription acne lotion, in the United States. Because Benzac, its other acne product, was about to lose U.S. patent protection, Galderma felt tremendous pressure to build Epiduo's U.S. market share as quickly as possible. But in Europe, the product had met stiff competition from Duac, an acne gel made by GlaxoSmithKline (GSK). Expecting more of the same in the United States, Galderma decided to implement a program to reimburse a patient's out-of-pocket costs for the product for as long as a year. In exchange for rebate coupons, customers gave the company their e-mail addresses. Galderma then sent them skin care tips, acne information, and special offers for its non-prescription products, such as cleansing bars.

Heavily rebating new drugs in the early days to build market share is a common strategy in the pharmaceutical industry. The hope is that once the company has won a substantial share, health insurance companies will agree to cover the drug, allowing the company to offset its development costs and make a profit before its patents expire.

But incumbents selling established drugs are generally unwilling to take risks with pricing. Their cost accounting systems and P&L structures make them feel that they must cover their substantial product costs—which explains why GSK and other incumbents seemed paralyzed when Galderma launched the rebate program for Epiduo. One GSK executive told us, "We can't afford to match them, and we can scarcely afford to discount. So we're losing share."

In reality, the marginal cost—the material and labor—of a tube of lotion or gel is small (from a few pennies to a few dollars). Therefore, in the short run incumbents would have lost almost nothing if they had deeply discounted their products or matched Galderma's rebate. Moreover, like Galderma, they could have cross-sold products and, by breaking down the walls around P&L centers, used profits from other highly successful products to subsidize short-term losses in dermatology. This would have forced Galderma into the untenable position of giving away its product without growing share. The battle is ongoing, but so far Galderma's strategy has allowed it to gain customers and profitably cross-sell products.

Because free-product strategies entail experimentation and, admittedly, some risk taking, embracing them may require a cultural shift. Strong executive leadership will be needed to build the case for mounting a competitive response, revamping organizational structures, and questioning cost accounting information. When a free offering is a threat, few strategies are available besides meeting free with free. Incumbents that spend too much time looking for some other killer strategy often only defer the inevitable. By taking decisive action as soon as the threat is clear, incumbents can survive and thrive.

Originally published in June 2011. Reprint R1106H

Why the Lean Start-Up Changes Everything

by Steve Blank

LAUNCHING A NEW ENTERPRISE—whether it's a tech start-up, a small business, or an initiative within a large corporation—has always been a hit-or-miss proposition. According to the decades-old formula, you write a business plan, pitch it to investors, assemble a team, introduce a product, and start selling as hard as you can. And somewhere in this sequence of events, you'll probably suffer a fatal setback. The odds are not with you: As new research by Harvard Business School's Shikhar Ghosh shows, 75% of all start-ups fail.

But recently an important countervailing force has emerged, one that can make the process of starting a company less risky. It's a methodology called the "lean start-up," and it favors experimentation over elaborate planning, customer feedback over intuition, and iterative design over traditional "big design up front" development. Although the methodology is just a few years old, its concepts—such as "minimum viable product" and "pivoting"—have quickly taken root in the start-up world, and business schools have already begun adapting their curricula to teach them.

The lean start-up movement hasn't gone totally mainstream, however, and we have yet to feel its full impact. In many ways it is roughly where the big data movement was five years ago— consisting mainly of a buzzword that's not yet widely understood, whose implications companies are just beginning to grasp. But as its practices spread, they're turning the conventional wisdom about entrepreneurship on its head. New ventures of all kinds are attempting to improve their chances of success by following its principles of failing fast and continually learning. And despite the methodology's name, in the long term some of its biggest payoffs may be gained by the *large* companies that embrace it.

In this article I'll offer a brief overview of lean start-up techniques and how they've evolved. Most important, I'll explain how, in combination with other business trends, they could ignite a new entrepreneurial economy.

The Fallacy of the Perfect Business Plan

According to conventional wisdom, the first thing every founder must do is create a business plan—a static document that describes the size of an opportunity, the problem to be solved, and the solution that the new venture will provide. Typically it includes a five-year forecast for income, profits, and cash flow. A business plan is essentially a research exercise written in isolation at a desk before an entrepreneur has even begun to build a product. The assumption is that it's possible to figure out most of the unknowns of a business in advance, before you raise money and actually execute the idea.

Once an entrepreneur with a convincing business plan obtains money from investors, he or she begins developing the product in a similarly insular fashion. Developers invest thousands of man-hours to get it ready for launch, with little if any customer input. Only after building and launching the product does the venture get substantial feedback from customers—when the sales force attempts to sell it. And too often, after months or even years of development, entrepreneurs learn the hard way that customers do not need or want most of the product's features.

After decades of watching thousands of start-ups follow this standard regimen, we've now learned at least three things:

1. Business plans rarely survive first contact with customers. As the boxer Mike Tyson once said about his opponents' prefight strategies: "Everybody has a plan until they get punched in the mouth."

Idea in Brief

Over the past few years, a new methodology for launching companies, called the "lean start-up," has begun to replace the old regimen.

Instead of executing business plans, operating in stealth mode, and releasing fully functional prototypes, young ventures are testing hypotheses, gathering early and frequent customer feedback, and showing "minimum viable products" to prospects. This new process recognizes that searching for a business model (which is the primary task facing a start-up) is entirely different from executing against that model (which is what established firms do).

Recently, business schools have begun to teach the methodology, which can also be learned at events such as Startup Weekend. Over time, lean start-up techniques could reduce the failure rate of new ventures and, in combination with other trends taking hold in the business world, launch a new, more entrepreneurial economy.

2. No one besides venture capitalists and the late Soviet Union requires five-year plans to forecast complete unknowns. These plans are generally fiction, and dreaming them up is almost always a waste of time.

3. Start-ups are not smaller versions of large companies. They do not unfold in accordance with master plans. The ones that ultimately succeed go quickly from failure to failure, all the while adapting, iterating on, and improving their initial ideas as they continually learn from customers.

One of the critical differences is that while existing companies *execute* a business model, start-ups *look* for one. This distinction is at the heart of the lean start-up approach. It shapes the lean definition of a start-up: a temporary organization designed to search for a repeatable and scalable business model.

The lean method has three key principles:

First, rather than engaging in months of planning and research, entrepreneurs accept that all they have on day one is a series of untested hypotheses—basically, good guesses. So instead of writing an intricate business plan, founders summarize their hypotheses in

Sketch out your hypotheses

The business model canvas lets you look at all nine building blocks of your business on one page. Each component of the business model contains a series of hypotheses that you need to test.

Key partners	Key activities	Value propositions	Customer relationships	Customer segments
Who are our key partners? Who are our key suppliers? Which key resources are we acquiring from our partners? Which key activities do partners perform?	What key activities do our value propositions require? Our distribution channels? Customer relationships? Revenue streams?	What value do we deliver to the customer? Which one of our customers' problems are we helping to solve? What bundles of products and services are we offering to each segment? Which customer needs are we satisfying? What is the minimum viable product?	How do we get, keep, and grow customers? Which customer relationships have we established? How are they integrated with the rest of our business model? How costly are they?	For whom are we creating value? Who are our most important customers? What are the customer archetypes?
	Key resources		**Channels**	
	What key resources do our value propositions require? Our distribution channels? Customer relationships? Revenue streams?		Through which channels do our customer segments want to be reached? How do other companies reach them now? Which ones work best? Which ones are most cost-efficient? How are we integrating them with customer routines?	

Cost structure		Revenue streams	
What are the most important costs inherent to our business model? Which key resources are most expensive? Which key activities are most expensive?		For what value are our customers really willing to pay? For what do they currently pay? What is the revenue model? What are the pricing tactics?	

Source: www.businessmodelgeneration.com/canvas. Canvas concept developed by Alexander Osterwalder and Yves Pigneur.

a framework called a *business model canvas*. Essentially, this is a diagram of how a company creates value for itself and its customers. (See the exhibit "Sketch out your hypotheses.")

Second, lean start-ups use a "get out of the building" approach called *customer development* to test their hypotheses. They go out and ask potential users, purchasers, and partners for feedback on all elements of the business model, including product features, pricing, distribution channels, and affordable customer acquisition strategies. The emphasis is on nimbleness and speed: New ventures rapidly assemble minimum viable products and immediately elicit customer feedback. Then, using customers' input to revise their assumptions, they start the cycle over again, testing redesigned offerings and making further small adjustments (iterations) or more substantive ones (pivots) to ideas that aren't working. (See the exhibit "Listen to customers.")

Third, lean start-ups practice something called *agile development*, which originated in the software industry. Agile development works hand-in-hand with customer development. Unlike typical yearlong product development cycles that presuppose knowledge of customers' problems and product needs, agile development eliminates wasted time and resources by developing the product iteratively and incrementally. It's the process by which start-ups create the minimum viable products they test. (See the exhibit "Quick, responsive development.")

When Jorge Heraud and Lee Redden started Blue River Technology, they were students in my class at Stanford. They had a vision of building robotic lawn mowers for commercial spaces. After talking to over 100 customers in 10 weeks, they learned their initial customer target—golf courses—didn't value their solution. But then they began to talk to farmers and found a huge demand for an automated way to kill weeds without chemicals. Filling it became their new product focus, and within 10 weeks Blue River had built and tested a prototype. Nine months later the start-up had obtained more than $3 million in venture funding. The team expected to have a commercial product ready just nine months after that.

Listen to customers

During customer development, a start-up searches for a business model that works. If customer feedback reveals that its business hypotheses are wrong, it either revises them or "pivots" to new hypotheses. Once a model is proven, the start-up starts executing, building a formal organization. Each stage of customer development is iterative: A start-up will probably fail several times before finding the right approach.

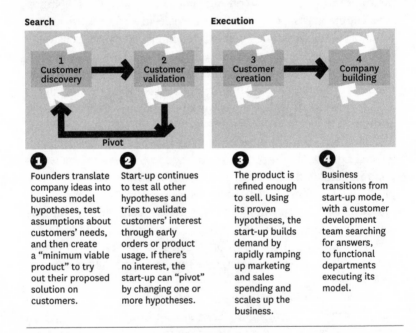

❶ Founders translate company ideas into business model hypotheses, test assumptions about customers' needs, and then create a "minimum viable product" to try out their proposed solution on customers.

❷ Start-up continues to test all other hypotheses and tries to validate customers' interest through early orders or product usage. If there's no interest, the start-up can "pivot" by changing one or more hypotheses.

❸ The product is refined enough to sell. Using its proven hypotheses, the start-up builds demand by rapidly ramping up marketing and sales spending and scales up the business.

❹ Business transitions from start-up mode, with a customer development team searching for answers, to functional departments executing its model.

Stealth Mode's Declining Popularity

Lean methods are changing the language start-ups use to describe their work. During the dot-com boom, start-ups often operated in "stealth mode" (to avoid alerting potential competitors to a market opportunity), exposing prototypes to customers only during highly orchestrated "beta" tests. The lean start-up methodology makes those concepts obsolete because it holds that in most industries

Quick, responsive development

In contrast to traditional product development, in which each stage occurs in linear order and lasts for months, agile development builds products in short, repeated cycles. A start-up produces a "minimum viable product"—containing only critical features—gathers feedback on it from customers, and then starts over with a revised minimum viable product.

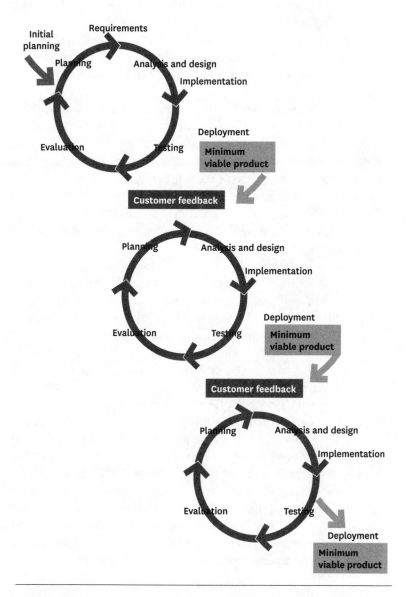

customer feedback matters more than secrecy and that constant feedback yields better results than cadenced unveilings.

Those two fundamental precepts crystallized for me during my career as an entrepreneur. (I've been involved with eight high-tech start-ups, as either a founder or an early employee.) When I shifted into teaching, a decade ago, I came up with the formula for customer development described earlier. By 2003 I was outlining this process in a course at the Haas School of Business at the University of California at Berkeley.

In 2004, I invested in a start-up founded by Eric Ries and Will Harvey and, as a condition of my investment, insisted that they take my course. Eric quickly recognized that waterfall development, the tech industry's traditional, linear product development approach, should be replaced by iterative agile techniques. He also saw similarities between this emerging set of start-up disciplines and the Toyota Production System, which had become known as "lean manufacturing." Eric dubbed the combination of customer development and agile practices the "lean start-up."

The tools were popularized by a series of successful books. In 2003, I wrote *The Four Steps to the Epiphany,* articulating for the first time that start-ups were not smaller versions of large companies and laying out the customer development process in detail. In 2010, Alexander Osterwalder and Yves Pigneur gave entrepreneurs the standard framework for business model canvases in *Business Model Generation.* In 2011 Eric published an overview in *The Lean Startup.* And in 2012 Bob Dorf and I summarized what we'd learned about lean techniques in a step-by-step handbook called *The Startup Owner's Manual.*

The lean start-up method is now being taught at more than 25 universities and through a popular online course at Udacity.com. In addition, in almost every city around world, you'll find organizations like Startup Weekend introducing the lean method to hundreds of prospective entrepreneurs at a time. At such gatherings a roomful of start-up teams can cycle through half a dozen potential product ideas in a matter of hours. Although it sounds incredible to people who haven't been to one, at these events some businesses are formed on a Friday evening and are generating actual revenue by Sunday afternoon.

Creating an Entrepreneurial, Innovation-Based Economy

While some adherents claim that the lean process can make individual start-ups more successful, I believe that claim is too grandiose. Success is predicated on too many factors for one methodology to guarantee that any single start-up will be a winner. But on the basis of what I've seen at hundreds of start-ups, at programs that teach lean principles, and at established companies that practice them, I can make a more important claim: Using lean methods across a portfolio of start-ups will result in fewer failures than using traditional methods.

A lower start-up failure rate could have profound economic consequences. Today the forces of disruption, globalization, and regulation are buffeting the economies of every country. Established industries are rapidly shedding jobs, many of which will never return. Employment growth in the 21st century will have to come from new ventures, so we all have a vested interest in fostering an environment that helps them succeed, grow, and hire more workers. The creation of an innovation economy that's driven by the rapid expansion of start-ups has never been more imperative.

In the past, growth in the number of start-ups was constrained by five factors in addition to the failure rate:

1. The high cost of getting the first customer and the even higher cost of getting the product wrong.

2. Long technology development cycles.

3. The limited number of people with an appetite for the risks inherent in founding or working at a start-up.

4. The structure of the venture capital industry, in which a small number of firms each needed to invest big sums in a handful of start-ups to have a chance at significant returns.

5. The concentration of real expertise in how to build start-ups, which in the United States was mostly found in pockets on the East and West coasts. (This is less an issue in Europe and other parts of the world, but even overseas there are geographic entrepreneurial hot spots.)

What Lean Start-Ups Do Differently

THE FOUNDERS OF LEAN START-UPS don't begin with a business plan; they begin with the search for a business model. Only after quick rounds of experimentation and feedback reveal a model that works do lean founders focus on execution.

Lean	Traditional
STRATEGY	
Business model Hypothesis-driven	**Business plan** Implementation-driven
NEW-PRODUCT PROCESS	
Customer development Get out of the office and test hypotheses	**Product management** Prepare offering for market following a linear, step-by-step plan
ENGINEERING	
Agile development Build the product iteratively and incrementally	**Agile or waterfall development** Build the product iteratively, or fully specify the product before building it
ORGANIZATION	
Customer and agile development teams Hire for learning, nimbleness, and speed	**Departments by function** Hire for experience and ability to execute
FINANCIAL REPORTING	
Metrics that matter Customer acquisition cost, lifetime customer value, churn, viralness	**Accounting** Income statement, balance sheet, cash flow statement
FAILURE	
Expected Fix by iterating on ideas and pivoting away from ones that don't work	**Exception** Fix by firing executives
SPEED	
Rapid Operates on good-enough data	**Measured** Operates on complete data

The lean approach reduces the first two constraints by helping new ventures launch products that customers actually want, far more quickly and cheaply than traditional methods, and the third by making start-ups less risky. And it has emerged at a time when other business and technology trends are likewise breaking down the barriers to start-up formation. The combination of all these forces is altering the entrepreneurial landscape.

Today open source software, like GitHub, and cloud services, such as Amazon Web Services, have slashed the cost of software development from millions of dollars to thousands. Hardware start-ups no longer have to build their own factories, since offshore manufacturers are so easily accessible. Indeed, it's become quite common to see young tech companies that practice the lean start-up methodology offer software products that are simply "bits" delivered over the web or hardware that's built in China within weeks of being formed. Consider Roominate, a start-up designed to inspire girls' confidence and interest in science, technology, engineering, and math. Once its founders had finished testing and iterating on the design of their wired dollhouse kit, they sent the specs off to a contract manufacturer in China. Three weeks later the first products arrived.

Another important trend is the decentralization of access to financing. Venture capital used to be a tight club of formal firms clustered near Silicon Valley, Boston, and New York. In today's entrepreneurial ecosystem, new super angel funds, smaller than the traditional hundred-million-dollar-sized VC fund, can make early-stage investments. Worldwide, hundreds of accelerators, like Y Combinator and TechStars, have begun to formalize seed investments. And crowdsourcing sites like Kickstarter provide another, more democratic method of financing start-ups.

The instantaneous availability of information is also a boon to today's new ventures. Before the internet, new company founders got advice only as often as they could have coffee with experienced investors or entrepreneurs. Today the biggest challenge is sorting through the overwhelming amount of start-up advice they get. The lean concepts provide a framework that helps you differentiate the good from the bad.

Lean start-up techniques were initially designed to create fast-growing tech ventures. But I believe the concepts are equally valid for creating the Main Street small businesses that make up the bulk of the economy. If the entire universe of small business embraced them, I strongly suspect it would increase growth and efficiency, and have a direct and immediate impact on GDP and employment.

There are signs that this may in fact happen. In 2011 the U.S. National Science Foundation began using lean methods to commercialize basic science research in a program called the Innovation Corps. Eleven universities now teach the methods to hundreds of teams of senior research scientists across the United States.

MBA programs are adopting these techniques, too. For years they taught students to apply large-company approaches—such as accounting methods for tracking revenue and cash flow, and organizational theories about managing—to start-ups. Yet start-ups face completely different issues. Now business schools are realizing that new ventures need their own management tools.

As business schools embrace the distinction between management execution and searching for a business model, they're abandoning the business plan as the template for entrepreneurial education. And the business plan competitions that have been a celebrated part of the MBA experience for over a decade are being replaced by business model competitions. (Harvard Business School became the latest to make this switch, in 2012.) Stanford, Harvard, Berkeley, and Columbia are leading the charge and embracing the lean start-up curriculum. My Lean LaunchPad course for educators is now training over 250 college and university instructors a year.

A New Strategy for the 21st-Century Corporation

It's already becoming clear that lean start-up practices are not just for young tech ventures.

Corporations have spent the past 20 years increasing their efficiency by driving down costs. But simply focusing on improving existing business models is not enough anymore. Almost every large company understands that it also needs to deal with ever-increasing external threats by continually innovating. To ensure their survival and growth, corporations need to keep inventing new business models. This challenge requires entirely new organizational structures and skills.

Over the years managerial experts such as Clayton Christensen, Rita McGrath, Vijay Govindarajan, Henry Chesbrough, Ian MacMillan, Alexander Osterwalder, and Eric von Hippel have advanced the thinking on how large companies can improve their innovation processes. During the past three years, however, we have seen large companies, including General Electric, Qualcomm, and Intuit, begin to implement the lean start-up methodology.

GE's Energy Storage division, for instance, is using the approach to transform the way it innovates. In 2010 Prescott Logan, the general manager of the division, recognized that a new battery developed by the unit had the potential to disrupt the industry. Instead of preparing to build a factory, scale up production, and launch the new offering (ultimately named Durathon) as a traditional product extension, Logan applied lean techniques. He started searching for a business model and engaging in customer discovery. He and his team met face-to-face with dozens of global prospects to explore potential new markets and applications. These weren't sales calls: The team members left their PowerPoint slides behind and listened to customers' issues and frustrations with the battery status quo. They dug deep to learn how customers bought industrial batteries, how often they used them, and the operating conditions. With this feedback, they made a major shift in their customer focus. They eliminated one of their initial target segments, data centers, and discovered a new one—utilities. In addition, they narrowed the broad customer segment of "telecom" to cell phone providers in developing countries with unreliable electric grids. Eventually GE invested $100 million to build a world-class battery manufacturing facility in Schenectady, New York, which it opened in 2012. According to press reports, demand for the new batteries is so high that GE is already running a backlog of orders.

The first hundred years of management education focused on building strategies and tools that formalized execution and efficiency for existing businesses. Now, we have the first set of tools for searching for new business models as we launch start-up ventures. It also happens to have arrived just in time to help existing companies deal with the forces of continual disruption. In the 21st century those forces will make people in every kind of organization—start-ups, small businesses, corporations, and government—feel the pressure of rapid change. The lean start-up approach will help them meet it head-on, innovate rapidly, and transform business as we know it.

Originally published in May 2013. Reprint R1305C

Finding the Platform in Your Product

by Andrei Hagiu and Elizabeth J. Altman

FIVE OF THE TEN MOST VALUABLE COMPANIES in the world today—Apple, Alphabet, Amazon, Facebook, and Microsoft—derive much of their worth from their multisided platforms (MSPs), which facilitate interactions or transactions between parties. Many MSPs are more valuable than companies in the same industries that provide only products or services: For instance, Airbnb is now worth more than Marriott, the world's largest hotel chain.

However, companies that weren't born as platform businesses rarely realize that they can—at least partially—turn their products and services into an MSP. And even if they do realize it, they often wander in the dark searching for a strategy to achieve this transformation. Here we provide a framework for doing so. It lays out four specific ways in which products and services can be turned into platforms and examines the strategic advantages and pitfalls of each. These ideas are applicable to physical as well as online businesses.

Why seek to transform products and services into MSPs in the first place? As one Intuit executive told us, it comes down to "fear and greed." Greed, of course, refers to the potential for new revenue sources that could speed growth and increase a company's value. Fear refers to the danger that existing and incoming competitors will steal market share from your product or service. Transforming an offering into a platform might enhance your company's competitive advantage and raise barriers to entry via network effects and higher switching costs. We're not suggesting that every company should try to emulate Airbnb, Alibaba, Facebook, or Uber. But many companies would benefit from adding elements of a platform business to their offerings.

Our goal is to help managers discern how their products or services could become multisided platforms—and what challenges and opportunities might arise—so that they can decide whether or not to make the change. Our framework derives from our combined experience studying and advising more than a dozen companies (including several mentioned below) during product-to-MSP transformations. Managers might want to use this article as the basis for a corporate-strategy offsite at which everyone is given the task of articulating MSP strategies around existing company offerings. That assignment should include answering questions such as: (1) Are there benefits to turning some or all of our products and services into MSPs? (2) Are there risks involved in doing so? (3) What key resources, relationships (including how we interact with customers), and organizational changes would be required for such a transformation?

The reason regular products and services are not multisided platforms is that they do not serve multiple groups or facilitate interactions between customers or groups. In this article we discuss four ways in which regular products and services can bridge this gap and become MSPs.

1. Opening the Door to Third Parties

In this scenario your product or service has a big customer base that third-party sellers of other offerings are interested in reaching. You become an MSP by making it possible for those third parties to connect with your customers. "Connect with" can mean advertise or sell (or both) to them. The third-party products may be independent of your product or service or may be apps or modules that work in combination with your offerings.

Idea in Brief

The Problem

Many companies that sell products or services either don't realize they could turn their offerings into a platform business or struggle to do so.

The Opportunity

By becoming a multisided platform (MSP) that facilitates interactions between parties, a company may be able to provide new revenue sources while also preventing competitors from stealing market share from its product or service.

The Solution

Here are four scenarios whereby regular products or services can become MSPs. The authors take into account the advantages and pitfalls of each and the resources, relationships, and organizational changes that would be required.

Consider three examples:

Intuit is the leading seller of financial management, accounting, and tax software products for consumers and small businesses in the United States. In the past six years or so it has taken significant steps to turn QuickBooks, its flagship financial-accounting product for small businesses, into an MSP. It opened up application-programming interfaces and introduced a developer program and an app store to allow third-party developers to build and sell software products to QuickBooks' customer base. Those products leverage data about small-business finances provided by QuickBooks. Since 2013 QuickBooks has also enabled its customers to apply directly to several third-party financial institutions for loans through a service called QuickBooks Financing.

Health clubs are increasingly renting space inside their gyms to specialty studios so that the latter can serve health club members. This allows a club to offer a greater variety of classes, which helps it retain existing members and attract new ones. For instance, the Forum Athletic Club, in Atlanta, recently reached an agreement with Cyc Fitness, a national cycling-studio chain, which now operates a self-contained studio inside the Forum's 22,000-square-foot gym.

The Lawson chain of convenience stores in Japan started in the 1990s to turn its shops into MSPs that facilitate transactions between its customers and third-party service providers. Today Lawson customers can pay utility bills and insurance premiums, ship and pick up parcels through postal service providers, and claim items ordered from e-commerce sites just by visiting their local convenience store.

For your product or service to become a true MSP in this scenario, at least some of the connection between your customers and third parties must be made through your product. Intuit could simply have sold aggregated (and anonymized) QuickBooks data to third-party developers and financial institutions. That would have added a potentially profitable new offering for Intuit, but it would not have turned QuickBooks into an MSP that could exploit network effects.

For this type of transition to make sense, your product or service must have an established brand and a large customer base—but that alone won't elicit interest from third parties. It must also meet one or both of the following conditions:

It serves a baseline need for many customers, yet leaves a large number of heterogeneous customer needs unserved. You can encourage and enable third parties to fill those gaps with products and services that are typically complementary to yours. Most third-party apps in Intuit's app store target market niches and customer needs not served by QuickBooks on its own.

It generates frequent customer interactions. That makes it a good candidate to become a one-stop shop for other, not necessarily complementary products and services. The third-party services that Lawson's customers can access are largely unrelated to its own products and services, but customers find it extremely convenient to access all of them in the same location.

It's important to be aware of several pitfalls associated with this approach to an MSP. One is that customers who come to you primarily for a product or service may object to the advertising of third-party offerings, especially if they are paying for yours. Intuit faced this when it started exploring services to offer through QuickBooks. As a result, the company is very careful to allow only offerings that align well with the needs and desires of QuickBooks customers and to obtain explicit consent to participate in tests for targeted third-party offers. In addition, Intuit has rebranded QuickBooks as "the operating system for small business" precisely to change customers' perceptions and to minimize potential backlash.

Another possible pitfall is that because you have an existing provider relationship with your customers, they may hold you responsible for the quality of their interactions with third parties. By enabling those parties to interact with your customers, you are implicitly endorsing their offerings—to a greater extent than does a company born as a multisided platform. For instance, a customer taking a spinning class offered by a third-party studio in a health club's gym is likely to blame the health club for a bad experience. As a result, you must curate third-party products and services much more carefully than a company born as an MSP has to.

Finally, some third-party products and services may cannibalize your offerings. The natural inclination would be to allow only those that are either complementary or unrelated to yours. But that approach can be misguided. In some cases it may make sense to coopt offerings that compete somewhat with yours and capture some of the resulting value to your customers. The Forum Athletic Club has replaced its own cycling classes with the Cyc Fitness classes offered at its gym. Cyc's spinning classes have proved more popular with members and allow the Forum to focus its resources on other services while converting Cyc from a competitor to a complementor.

The underlying logic is that if substitution from third parties is inevitable, bringing them onto your platform may expand its overall appeal to your customers, resulting in more demand and opportunities to sell your own services. It may also encourage you to reevaluate your offering's core competitive advantages and focus on them, which may mean ceding ground to third parties in some areas.

2. Connecting Customers

In this scenario you are selling a product or service to two distinct customer segments that interact or transact with each other outside your offering. You can become an MSP by modifying or expanding your offering so that at least some element of those interactions or transactions occurs through your product or service.

Quickbooks is used by both small businesses and accounting professionals. Intuit is in the process of adding a matchmaking function within QuickBooks that would enable small businesses to find and contact accountants with relevant expertise in their geographic area and would allow already-matched business-accountant pairs to exchange documents through the product.

Garmin and other fitness wearables are used by both consumers and personal trainers. Many companies that offer these products also host online systems (Garmin Connect, for example) to store fitness-training and health data. Garmin could enable users to share their data with personal trainers, thereby enhancing the interactions between those two groups. To further capture value from this strategy, Garmin could charge trainers for a "pro" subscription—software tools that would let them access clients' data to oversee activities and progress. This scenario highlights how different customer segments of the same product or service can become customer groups on an MSP. For example, men and women are customer segments for a hair salon (no interaction between them is facilitated by the salon), but they are customer groups for a heterosexual dating service. An entrepreneurial hair salon that started offering matchmaking services to its customer segments could convert men and women into customer groups.

There are two pitfalls associated with this strategy. First, you run the risk of wasting resources on a feature that ultimately creates little additional value for your customers or your company. Worse, the MSP feature can be a detriment if customers perceive it as misaligned with the value of your underlying product or service. Some customers of a hair salon that provides matchmaking services might not want to risk encountering matches that didn't work out. Others might worry that offering a dating service means the salon isn't focused on giving the highest-quality haircuts.

Blizzard Entertainment's ill-fated Auction House for its popular Diablo video game provides a cautionary tale. Having noticed that Diablo players were routinely trading digital items on eBay and other external platforms, Blizzard created the Auction House in 2012 to make those transactions easier. It allowed players to buy and sell digital items in exchange for "gold" (digital currency in the Diablo game) as well as real dollars—and Blizzard was able to charge a transaction fee. It quickly became clear, however, that this feature created perverse incentives. Many players decided that buying items at the Auction House was an easier way to reach the game's advanced stages than devoting several hours to killing monsters and searching for loot inside the game. Other players strove to accumulate game items for the sole purpose of selling them in the Auction House. Realizing that this behavior was undermining the value of the game itself, Blizzard shut down the Auction House in 2014.

———————

It is imperative that you conduct market research or run experiments to answer the following questions: Would significant proportions of our offering's various customer segments derive substantial benefits from interacting or transacting with one another? If yes, can our product or service enhance those interactions in a significant way? How will our customers react to the addition of an MSP feature, and how will that feature affect the way they interact with the original offering?

The second pitfall, as in scenario number one, is that although your offering is now simply facilitating a connection or a transaction between two parties, if one party is dissatisfied with the other, you may be held partly responsible. That means you need to put governance mechanisms in place to minimize (if not eliminate) the likelihood of unsatisfactory interactions. Intuit will have to carefully curate the accountants it recommends to QuickBooks customers through its matchmaking feature.

3. Connecting Products to Connect Customers

In this scenario you are selling two products or services, each to a different customer base, and the two customer bases interact outside your offerings. You can become an MSP by modifying or expanding your offerings so that at least part of those interactions occurs through one or both of your offerings.

Cards Against Humanity is a popular game in which players complete fill-in-the-blank statements with humorous (and often tasteless) words or phrases printed on physical playing cards. Its creators continue to sell the game and its numerous expansion packs to consumers, but they have also created Blackbox, a separate website through which they sell back-end fulfillment services (credit-card processing, customer service, shipping) to independent artists who want to sell their products—including third-party developers of other card games. Currently these are separate offerings, but the company could create an MSP by linking them. For instance, it could allow Blackbox customers to advertise their games to Cards Against Humanity's users with expansion packs. A more sophisticated implementation would allow Blackbox customers to test game concepts on willing Cards Against Humanity users, who would provide feedback.

Credit bureaus such as Equifax, Experian, and TransUnion offer a suite of services for consumers (access to credit scores, identity theft protection, and so on) and a suite of services for financial institutions (credit reports on consumers and businesses). These suites are based on the same data, but the two types of customers interact outside the services (as when a consumer applies for a mortgage); the credit bureaus do not directly facilitate those interactions.

Credit bureaus could create online MSPs where consumers could obtain their credit scores and receive targeted offers from financial institutions. (This is the business model of start-ups such as Credit Karma and Lendio.) These MSPs could go further and enable consumers to create and manage a digital data profile that they could then use to apply directly for financial products at participating institutions (similar to the way Intuit allows QuickBooks customers to apply for financial products through QuickBooks Financing).

Nielsen offers "watch" products to media companies (data on consumers' viewing habits) and "buy" products to consumer goods manufacturers (data on consumers' purchasing habits). One could easily imagine Nielsen's adding the ability for a consumer-packaged-goods company to connect with relevant media companies for advertising purposes.

This scenario highlights how a multiproduct company can become a multisided platform that benefits from network effects. For example, by increasing sales of credit and identity-theft-protection products to consumers, credit bureaus can improve their offerings for financial institutions (which leverage consumer data), thereby achieving greater cross-product economies of scope. While that alone might be valuable, credit bureaus could create and capture even more value by linking the two kinds of products to facilitate interactions between consumers and financial institutions (as described above). This would create an MSP and generate network effects: If more consumers use the credit and identity-theft-protection products, that increases the value of the offerings for financial institutions, which can then transact with more consumers more effectively and vice versa.

Two risks are associated with this strategy. First, as with scenario number two, you may waste resources on a feature that ultimately creates little value for your customers or your company relative to the underlying product or service. Second, optimizing for interactions between customers of different products may lead to design choices that limit the growth potential of one or the other product on its own. Once again, it is imperative to use market research and experiments to answer a few questions: Would considerable proportions of your offerings' respective customers derive significantly greater benefits from interacting or transacting through you? If yes, can your offerings substantially enhance those interactions? How will the customers of your two offerings react to the addition of an MSP feature? How will that feature affect the way customers interact with the original products?

4. Supplying to a Multisided Platform

In this scenario you become an MSP by creating an offering for your customers' customers that enhances the value of the product or service they buy from your customers. (Although this strategy is logically possible, we are not yet aware of examples of its successful implementation.)

It is important to emphasize that this strategy goes beyond the more traditional "ingredient brand" strategy, which is also a "customers' customers" approach. Indeed, some (essential) ingredient suppliers have created brands in the eyes of their customers' customers (for example, Intel's "Intel Inside") that allow them to extract more value from their customers. But because these ingredient suppliers offer no products or services directly to their customers' customers, they are not MSPs.

The major pitfall with this scenario is that your customers are likely to react negatively to any attempt to go after their customers. Nevertheless, we believe this strategy could work under certain circumstances. The key is to convince your customers that the product or service you provide to their customers is truly complementary to—rather than competitive with—their own offerings.

Shopify is a leading provider of e-commerce tools to online and retail merchants. Currently the company has no direct connection with its customers' users. It could, however, start offering a common log-in or loyalty program to users of its customers' sites. Whether such an initiative would be successful would hinge on whether Shopify could persuade its merchant customers that the offering was a valuable added service rather than simply an attempt to take control of their customer relationships.

The decision whether and how to convert an offering into an MSP should be informed by who your current customers are, how you currently interact with them, and how they interact with one another. The most fundamental challenge associated with this endeavor is transitioning from a world in which you have 100% control over what your customers are offered to one in which you can only influence the value that is created for them (by third parties or by interactions among themselves).

A final consideration is organizational and leadership challenges. If a company has a solid reputation that is rooted in creating and offering products, shifting to an MSP-focused strategy might be difficult for employees who deeply identify with those products. And companies that sell successful products or services often have strong research and development operations and many engineers in leadership roles; shifting to an MSP strategy that depends on the adept management of third-party relationships might require putting business-development and marketing professionals in significant leadership roles, generating internal conflict. Furthermore, as a company's strategy moves from a product or service orientation to being more MSP-centric, boards, CEOs, and senior management teams may find it difficult to deal with multiple or hybrid strategies, adopt and track new performance metrics, and enforce some degree of technological or customer experience consistency between previously separate products and services.

Nevertheless, if you decide that creating a platform will provide great opportunities for growth and increased profitability and thwart potential competitive threats, the effort to make the transformation may well be worthwhile.

Originally published in July–August 2017. Reprint R1704G

Pipelines, Platforms, and the New Rules of Strategy

by Marshall W. Van Alstyne, Geoffrey G. Parker, and Sangeet Paul Choudary

BACK IN 2007 the five major mobile-phone manufacturers—Nokia, Samsung, Motorola, Sony Ericsson, and LG—collectively controlled 90% of the industry's global profits. That year, Apple's iPhone burst onto the scene and began gobbling up market share.

By 2015 the iPhone *singlehandedly* generated 92% of global profits, while all but one of the former incumbents made no profit at all.

How can we explain the iPhone's rapid domination of its industry? And how can we explain its competitors' free fall? Nokia and the others had classic strategic advantages that should have protected them: strong product differentiation, trusted brands, leading operating systems, excellent logistics, protective regulation, huge R&D budgets, and massive scale. For the most part, those firms looked stable, profitable, and well entrenched.

Certainly the iPhone had an innovative design and novel capabilities. But in 2007, Apple was a weak, nonthreatening player surrounded by 800-pound gorillas. It had less than 4% of market share in desktop operating systems and none at all in mobile phones.

As we'll explain, Apple (along with Google's competing Android system) overran the incumbents by exploiting the power of platforms and leveraging the new rules of strategy they give rise to. Platform businesses bring together producers and consumers in high-value exchanges. Their chief assets are information and interactions, which together are also the source of the value they create and their competitive advantage.

Understanding this, Apple conceived the iPhone and its operating system as more than a product or a conduit for services. It imagined them as a way to connect participants in two-sided markets—app developers on one side and app users on the other—generating value for both groups. As the number of participants on each side grew, that value increased—a phenomenon called "network effects," which is central to platform strategy. By January 2015 the company's App Store offered 1.4 million apps and had cumulatively generated $25 billion for developers.

Apple's success in building a platform business within a conventional product firm holds critical lessons for companies across industries. Firms that fail to create platforms and don't learn the new rules of strategy will be unable to compete for long.

Pipeline to Platform

Platforms have existed for years. Malls link consumers and merchants; newspapers connect subscribers and advertisers. What's changed in this century is that information technology has profoundly reduced the need to own physical infrastructure and assets. IT makes building and scaling up platforms vastly simpler and cheaper, allows nearly frictionless participation that strengthens network effects, and enhances the ability to capture, analyze, and exchange huge amounts of data that increase the platform's value to all. You don't need to look far to see examples of platform businesses, from Uber to Alibaba to Airbnb, whose spectacular growth abruptly upended their industries.

Though they come in many varieties, platforms all have an ecosystem with the same basic structure, comprising four types of players. The *owners* of platforms control their intellectual property and governance. *Providers* serve as the platforms' interface with users.

Idea in Brief

The Sea Change

Platform businesses that bring together producers and consumers, as Uber and Airbnb do, are gobbling up market share and transforming competition. Traditional businesses that fail to create platforms and to learn the new rules of strategy will struggle.

The New Rules

With a platform, the critical asset is the community and the resources of its members. The focus of strategy shifts from controlling to orchestrating resources, from optimizing internal processes to facilitating external interactions, and from increasing customer value to maximizing ecosystem value.

The Upshot

In this new world, competition can emerge from seemingly unrelated industries or from within the platform itself. Firms must make smart choices about whom to let onto platforms and what they're allowed to do there, and must track new metrics designed to monitor and boost platform interactions.

Producers create their offerings, and *consumers* use those offerings. (See the exhibit "The players in a platform ecosystem.")

To understand how the rise of platforms is transforming competition, we need to examine how platforms differ from the conventional "pipeline" businesses that have dominated industry for decades. Pipeline businesses create value by controlling a linear series of activities—the classic value-chain model. Inputs at one end of the chain (say, materials from suppliers) undergo a series of steps that transform them into an output that's worth more: the finished product. Apple's handset business is essentially a pipeline. But combine it with the App Store, the marketplace that connects app developers and iPhone owners, and you've got a platform.

As Apple demonstrates, firms needn't be only a pipeline or a platform; they can be both. While plenty of pure pipeline businesses are still highly competitive, when platforms enter the same marketplace, the platforms virtually always win. That's why pipeline giants such as Walmart, Nike, John Deere, and GE are all scrambling to incorporate platforms into their models.

The players in a platform ecosystem

A platform provides the infrastructure and rules for a marketplace that brings together producers and consumers. The players in the ecosystem fill four main roles but may shift rapidly from one role to another. Understanding the relationships both within and outside the ecosystem is central to platform strategy.

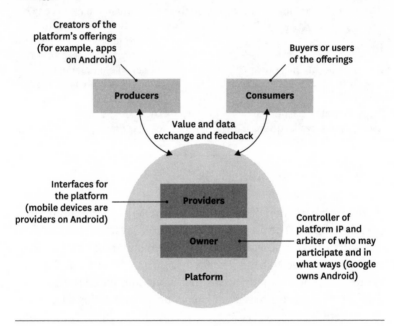

The move from pipeline to platform involves three key shifts:

1. From resource control to resource orchestration. The resource-based view of competition holds that firms gain advantage by controlling scarce and valuable—ideally, inimitable—assets. In a pipeline world, those include tangible assets such as mines and real estate and intangible assets like intellectual property. With platforms, the assets that are hard to copy are the community and the resources its members own and contribute, be they rooms or cars or ideas and information. In other words, the network of producers and consumers is the chief asset.

2. From internal optimization to external interaction. Pipeline firms organize their internal labor and resources to create value by optimizing an entire chain of product activities, from materials sourcing to sales and service. Platforms create value by facilitating interactions between external producers and consumers. Because of this external orientation, they often shed even variable costs of production. The emphasis shifts from dictating processes to persuading participants, and ecosystem governance becomes an essential skill.

3. From a focus on customer value to a focus on ecosystem value. Pipelines seek to maximize the lifetime value of individual customers of products and services, who, in effect, sit at the end of a linear process. By contrast, platforms seek to maximize the total value of an expanding ecosystem in a circular, iterative, feedback-driven process. Sometimes that requires subsidizing one type of consumer in order to attract another type.

These three shifts make clear that competition is more complicated and dynamic in a platform world. The competitive forces described by Michael Porter (the threat of new entrants and substitute products or services, the bargaining power of customers and suppliers, and the intensity of competitive rivalry) still apply. But on platforms these forces behave differently, and new factors come into play. To manage them, executives must pay close attention to the interactions on the platform, participants' access, and new performance metrics.

We'll examine each of these in turn. But first let's look more closely at network effects—the driving force behind every successful platform.

The Power of Network Effects

The engine of the industrial economy was, and remains, supply-side economies of scale. Massive fixed costs and low marginal costs mean that firms achieving higher sales volume than their competitors have a lower average cost of doing business. That allows them to reduce prices, which increases volume further, which permits more price cuts—a virtuous feedback loop that produces monopolies. Supply economics gave us Carnegie Steel, Edison Electric (which became GE), Rockefeller's Standard Oil, and many other industrial era giants.

In supply-side economies, firms achieve market power by controlling resources, ruthlessly increasing efficiency, and fending off challenges from any of the five forces. The goal of strategy in this world is to build a moat around the business that protects it from competition and channels competition toward other firms.

The driving force behind the internet economy, conversely, is demand-side economies of scale, also known as network effects. These are enhanced by technologies that create efficiencies in social networking, demand aggregation, app development, and other phenomena that help networks expand. In the internet economy, firms that achieve higher "volume" than competitors (that is, attract more platform participants) offer a higher average value per transaction. That's because the larger the network, the better the matches between supply and demand and the richer the data that can be used to find matches. Greater scale generates more value, which attracts more participants, which creates more value—another virtuous feedback loop that produces monopolies. Network effects gave us Alibaba, which accounts for over 75% of Chinese e-commerce transactions; Google, which accounts for 82% of mobile operating systems and 94% of mobile search; and Facebook, the world's dominant social platform.

The five forces model doesn't factor in network effects and the value they create. It regards external forces as "depletive," or extracting value from a firm, and so argues for building barriers against them. In demand-side economies, however, external forces can be "accretive"—adding value to the platform business. Thus the power of suppliers and customers, which is threatening in a supply-side world, may be viewed as an asset on platforms. Understanding when external forces may either add or extract value in an ecosystem is central to platform strategy.

How Platforms Change Strategy

In pipeline businesses, the five forces are relatively defined and stable. If you're a cement manufacturer or an airline, your customers and competitive set are fairly well understood, and the boundaries separating your suppliers, customers, and competitors are reasonably clear. In platform businesses, those boundaries can shift rapidly, as we'll discuss.

Forces within the ecosystem

Platform participants—consumers, producers, and providers—typically create value for a business. But they may defect if they believe their needs can be met better elsewhere. More worrisome, they may turn on the platform and compete directly with it. Zynga began as a games producer on Facebook but then sought to migrate players onto its own platform. Amazon and Samsung, providers of devices for the Android platform, tried to create their own versions of the operating system and take consumers with them.

The new roles that players assume can be either accretive or depletive. For example, consumers and producers can swap roles in ways that generate value for the platform. Users can ride with Uber today and drive for it tomorrow; travelers can stay with Airbnb one night and serve as hosts for other customers the next. In contrast, providers on a platform may become depletive, especially if they decide to compete with the owner. Netflix, a provider on the platforms of telecommunication firms, has control of consumers' interactions with the content it offers, so it can extract value from the platform owners while continuing to rely on their infrastructure.

As a consequence, platform firms must constantly encourage accretive activity within their ecosystems while monitoring participants' activity that may prove depletive. This is a delicate governance challenge that we'll discuss further.

Forces exerted by ecosystems

Managers of pipeline businesses can fail to anticipate platform competition from seemingly unrelated industries. Yet successful platform businesses tend to move aggressively into new terrain

Networks Invert the Firm

PIPELINE FIRMS HAVE LONG outsourced aspects of their internal functions, such as customer service. But today companies are taking that shift even further, moving toward orchestrating external networks that can complement or entirely replace the activities of once-internal functions.

Inversion extends outsourcing: Where firms might once have furnished design specifications to a known supplier, they now tap ideas they haven't yet imagined from third parties they don't even know. Firms are being turned inside out as value-creating activities move beyond their direct control and their organizational boundaries.

Marketing is no longer just about creating internally managed outbound messages. It now extends to the creation and propagation of messages by consumers themselves. Travel destination marketers invite consumers to submit videos of their trips and promote them on social media. The online eyeglasses retailer Warby Parker encourages consumers to post online photos of themselves modeling different styles and ask friends to help them choose. Consumers get more-flattering glasses, and Warby Parker gets viral exposure.

Information technology, historically focused on managing internal enterprise systems, increasingly supports external social and community networks. Threadless, a producer of T-shirts, coordinates communication not just to and from but among customers, who collaborate to develop the best product designs.

---

and into what were once considered separate industries with little warning. Google has moved from web search into mapping, mobile operating systems, home automation, driverless cars, and voice recognition. As a result of such shape-shifting, a platform can abruptly transform an incumbent's set of competitors. Swatch knows how to compete with Timex on watches but now must also compete with Apple. Siemens knows how to compete with Honeywell in thermostats but now is being challenged by Google's Nest.

Competitive threats tend to follow one of three patterns. First, they may come from an established platform with superior network effects that uses its relationships with customers to enter your industry. Products have features; platforms have communities, and those communities can be leveraged. Given Google's relation-

Human resources functions at companies increasingly leverage the wisdom of networks to augment internal talent. Enterprise software giant SAP has opened the internal system on which its developers exchange problems and solutions to its external ecosystem—to developers at both its own partners and its partners' clients. Information sharing across this network has improved product development and productivity and reduced support costs.

Finance, which historically has recorded its activities on private internal accounts, now records some transactions externally on public, or "distributed," ledgers. Organizations such as IBM, Intel, and JPMorgan are adopting blockchain technology that allows ledgers to be securely shared and vetted by anyone with permission. Participants can inspect everything from aggregated accounts to individual transactions. This allows firms to, for example, crowdsource compliance with accounting principles or seek input on their financial management from a broad network outside the company. Opening the books this way taps the wisdom of crowds and signals trustworthiness.

Operations and logistics traditionally emphasize the management of just-in-time inventory. More and more often, that function is being supplanted by the management of "not-even-mine" inventory—whether rooms, apps, or other assets owned by network participants. Indeed, if Marriott, Yellow Cab, and NBC had added platforms to their pipeline value chains, then Airbnb, Uber, and YouTube might never have come into being.

ship with consumers, the value its network provides them, and its interest in the internet of things, Siemens might have predicted the tech giant's entry into the home-automation market (though not necessarily into thermostats). Second, a competitor may target an overlapping customer base with a distinctive new offering that leverages network effects. Airbnb's and Uber's challenges to the hotel and taxi industries fall into this category. The final pattern, in which platforms that collect the same type of data that your firm does suddenly go after your market, is still emerging. When a data set is valuable, but different parties control different chunks of it, competition between unlikely camps may ensue. This is happening in health care, where traditional providers, producers of wearables like Fitbit, and retail pharmacies like Walgreens are all launching platforms based on the health data they own. They can be expected to compete for control of a broader data set—and the consumer relationships that come with it.

Focus

Managers of pipeline businesses focus on growing sales. For them, goods and services delivered (and the revenues and profits from them) are the units of analysis. For platforms, the focus shifts to interactions—exchanges of value between producers and consumers on the platform. The unit of exchange (say, a view of a video or a thumbs-up on a post) can be so small that little or no money changes hands. Nevertheless, the number of interactions and the associated network effects are the ultimate source of competitive advantage.

With platforms, a critical strategic aim is strong up-front design that will attract the desired participants, enable the right interactions (so-called core interactions), and encourage ever-more-powerful network effects. In our experience, managers often fumble here by focusing too much on the wrong type of interaction. And the perhaps counterintuitive bottom line, given how much we stress the importance of network effects, is that it's usually wise to ensure the value of interactions for participants before focusing on volume.

Most successful platforms launch with a single type of interaction that generates high value even if, at first, low volume. They then move into adjacent markets or adjacent types of interactions, increasing both value and volume. Facebook, for example, launched with a narrow focus (connecting Harvard students to other Harvard students) and then opened the platform to college students broadly and ultimately to everyone. LinkedIn launched as a professional networking site and later entered new markets with recruitment, publishing, and other offerings.

Access and governance

In a pipeline world, strategy revolves around erecting barriers. With platforms, while guarding against threats remains critical, the focus of strategy shifts to eliminating barriers to production and consumption in order to maximize value creation. To that end,

Harnessing Spillovers

POSITIVE SPILLOVER EFFECTS help platforms rapidly increase the volume of interactions. Book purchases on a platform, for example, generate book recommendations that create value for other participants on it, who then buy more books. This dynamic exploits the fact that network effects are often strongest among interactions of the same type (say, book sales) than among unrelated interactions (say, package pickup and yardwork in different cities mediated by the odd-job platform TaskRabbit).

Consider ride sharing. By itself, an individual ride on Uber is high value for both rider and driver—a desirable core interaction. As the number of platform participants increases, so does the value Uber delivers to both sides of the market; it becomes easier for consumers to get rides and for drivers to find fares. Spillover effects further enhance the value of Uber to participants: Data from riders' interactions with drivers—ratings of drivers and riders—improves the value of the platform to other users. Similarly, data on how well a given ride matched a rider's needs helps determine optimal pricing across the platform—another important spillover effect.

platform executives must make smart choices about access (whom to let onto the platform) and governance (or "control"—what consumers, producers, providers, and even competitors are allowed to do there).

Platforms consist of rules and architecture. Their owners need to decide how open both should be. An *open architecture* allows players to access platform resources, such as app developer tools, and create new sources of value. *Open governance* allows players other than the owner to shape the rules of trade and reward sharing on the platform. Regardless of who sets the rules, a fair reward system is key. If managers open the architecture but do not share the rewards, potential platform participants (such as app developers) have the ability to engage but no incentives. If managers open the rules and rewards but keep the architecture relatively closed, potential participants have incentives to engage but not the ability.

These choices aren't fixed. Platforms often launch with a fairly closed architecture and governance and then open up as they introduce new types of interactions and sources of value. But every platform must induce producers and consumers to interact and share their ideas and resources. Effective governance will inspire outsiders to bring valuable intellectual property to the platform, as Zynga did in bringing FarmVille to Facebook. That won't happen if prospective partners fear exploitation.

Some platforms encourage producers to create high-value offerings on them by establishing a policy of "permissionless innovation." They let producers invent things for the platform without approval but guarantee the producers will share in the value created. Rovio, for example, didn't need permission to create the Angry Birds game on the Apple operating system and could be confident that Apple wouldn't steal its IP. The result was a hit that generated enormous value for all participants on the platform. However, Google's Android platform has allowed even more innovation to flourish by being more open at the provider layer. That decision is one reason Google's market capitalization surpassed Apple's in early 2016 (just as Microsoft's did in the 1980s).

However, unfettered access can destroy value by creating "noise"—misbehavior or excess or low-quality content that inhibits interaction. One company that ran into this problem was Chatroulette, which paired random people from around the world for webchats. It grew exponentially until noise caused its abrupt collapse. Initially utterly open—it had no access rules at all—it soon encountered the "naked hairy man" problem, which is exactly what it sounds like. Clothed users abandoned the platform in droves. Chatroulette responded by reducing its openness with a variety of user filters.

Most successful platforms similarly manage openness to maximize positive network effects. Airbnb and Uber rate and insure hosts and drivers, Twitter and Facebook provide users with tools to prevent stalking, and Apple's App Store and the Google Play store both filter out low-quality applications.

Metrics

Leaders of pipeline enterprises have long focused on a narrow set of metrics that capture the health of their businesses. For example, pipelines grow by optimizing processes and opening bottlenecks;

one standard metric, inventory turnover, tracks the flow of goods and services through them. Push enough goods through and get margins high enough, and you'll see a reasonable rate of return.

As pipelines launch platforms, however, the numbers to watch change. Monitoring and boosting the performance of core interactions becomes critical. Here are new metrics managers need to track:

Interaction failure. If a traveler opens the Lyft app and sees "no cars available," the platform has failed to match an intent to consume with supply. Failures like these directly diminish network effects. Passengers who see this message too often will stop using Lyft, leading to higher driver downtimes, which can cause drivers to quit Lyft, resulting in even lower ride availability. Feedback loops can strengthen or weaken a platform.

Engagement. Healthy platforms track the participation of ecosystem members that enhances network effects—activities such as content sharing and repeat visits. Facebook, for example, watches the ratio of daily to monthly users to gauge the effectiveness of its efforts to increase engagement.

Match quality. Poor matches between the needs of users and producers weaken network effects. Google constantly monitors users' clicking and reading to refine how its search results fill their requests.

Negative network effects. Badly managed platforms often suffer from other kinds of problems that create negative feedback loops and reduce value. For example, congestion caused by unconstrained network growth can discourage participation. So can misbehavior, as Chatroulette found. Managers must watch for negative network effects and use governance tools to stem them by, for example, withholding privileges or banishing troublemakers.

Finally, platforms must understand the financial value of their communities and their network effects. Consider that in 2016, private equity markets placed the value of Uber, a demand economy firm founded in 2009, above that of GM, a supply economy firm founded in 1908. Clearly Uber's investors were looking beyond the traditional financials and metrics when calculating the firm's worth and potential. This is a clear indication that the rules have changed.

Because platforms require new approaches to strategy, they also demand new leadership styles. The skills it takes to tightly control internal resources just don't apply to the job of nurturing external ecosystems.

While pure platforms naturally launch with an external orientation, traditional pipeline firms must develop new core competencies—and a new mindset—to design, govern, and nimbly expand platforms on top of their existing businesses. The inability to make this leap explains why some traditional business leaders with impressive track records falter in platforms. Media mogul Rupert Murdoch bought the social network Myspace and managed it the way he might have run a newspaper—from the top down, bureaucratically, and with a focus more on controlling the internal operation than on fostering the ecosystem and creating value for participants. In time the Myspace community dissipated and the platform withered.

The failure to transition to a new approach explains the precarious situation that traditional businesses—from hotels to health care providers to taxis—find themselves in. For pipeline firms, the writing is on the wall: Learn the new rules of strategy for a platform world, or begin planning your exit.

Originally published in April 2016. Reprint R1604C

When One Business Model Isn't Enough

by Ramon Casadesus-Masanell and Jorge Tarziján

TRYING TO OPERATE MORE THAN one business model at a time is devilishly difficult—and frequently cited as a leading cause of strategic failure. Yet situations abound where a company may wish or need to address several customer segments, using a particular business model for each one. To crowd out competitors or forestall potential disruptors in its current markets, to expand into new markets, to make more efficient use of fixed assets and other resources, or to develop new income streams may all ideally require distinct business models that operate in tandem.

IBM and Compaq, for instance, supplemented their reseller distribution model with a direct-sell model to counteract Dell's growth in the 1990s. Netflix runs two business models for its DVD-by-mail and its streaming-video services. In emerging markets a bank sometimes creates a separate company to offer credit to low and middle-income customers, as Banco Santander-Chile has done with Banefe. The forestry company Celulosa Arauco turns its trees into paper pulp under one business model and into wood panels for high-end furniture under another.

Nowhere have the perils of running tandem business models been more evident than in the airline industry, where so many full-service carriers have met with so little success in introducing no-frills offerings to compete with low-cost competitors such as EasyJet and Southwest. Witness what happened to British Airways' Go Fly, Continental Lite, KLM's Buzz, and Delta's Song.

That's what makes the case of LAN Airlines, which success-fully operates three business models at once, so remarkable. The Chilean carrier has thrived by integrating a full-service international passenger-airline business model with an air-cargo business model while separately operating a no-frills passenger model for domestic flights. In fact, the word "thrived" is too modest: From 1993 to 2010, LAN posted 17% compound annual revenue growth through good times and bad (from $318 million in 1993 to $4.2 billion in 2010), while steadily raising annual net profits from zero to $420 million. LAN's market capitalization, at $8.9 billion as of March 11, 2011, ex-ceeds that of most of its main global rivals—US Airways ($1.5 billion), American Airlines ($2.2 billion), Korean Air ($3.7 billion), British Airways ($6.9 billion), and United-Continental ($8.1 billion). It even tops that of upstart Ryanair ($6.9 billion) and every other Latin American airline. From 1998 to 2010 LAN's share price, adjusted by dividends and splits, has grown by more than 1,500%.

LAN Airlines has succeeded where its rivals have not through a more subtle appreciation of the way different business models relate to one another. Certainly, many business models conflict, as in Netflix's high-profile case. Others, like the models for digital and film photography, are clear substitutes for each other. No doubt such models should be operated separately, and perhaps, only sequentially.

As LAN Airlines' experience makes clear, however, other busi-ness models are complementary. Indeed, they may be so mutually reinforcing that together they turn otherwise unviable possibilities into profitable opportunities. A company that recognizes which models are substitutes that must be kept separate and which are complements that strengthen each other can build a uniquely sustainable competitive advantage. Let's look at how LAN has used that insight to its benefit.

How LAN's Three Models Interrelate

LAN operates its full-service international passenger-carrier business in much the same way as other global carriers do. It offers frequent flights to major destinations through its own hubs and via

Idea in Brief

Trying to operate two business models at once often causes strategic failure. Yet LAN Airlines, a Chilean carrier, runs *three* models successfully. LAN has integrated a full-service international passenger model with a premium air-cargo business model while separately operating a no-frills passenger model for domestic flights.

LAN's multimodel success comes from recognizing the complementarity of its two high-end services and the distinct, or substitute, nature of its no-frills offering. LAN came to that insight by analyzing the major assets that the models share and the compatibility of the models' operational resources and capabilities. It recognized

that the more the models have in common, the more likely they are to generate greater value together than apart; the less they share, the more likely they are to be best executed separately.

Nevertheless, managing multiple models is a tall order. LAN has had to face greater complexity, broaden its organizational skills, increase the flexibility of its workforce, and make other investments. But by mastering three models, the company has built formidable advantages that are difficult for competitors to overcome. Its example has shown how, properly applied, the implementation of multiple business models is not a risk but rather a new tool for strategists.

alliances with other airlines. It has two classes (coach and business) of amenity-filled service, featuring complimentary hot meals and beverages, multilingual personal-entertainment units in coach, and fully flat beds in business class. Likewise, its no-frills domestic operation has essential elements in common with Southwest's and Ryanair's: It is a lower-cost, lower-overhead model characterized by fewer amenities, internet ticketing, shorter turnaround times, and a uniform fleet of single-aisle planes from which the kitchens have been removed to increase seating capacity.

What sets LAN apart is its cargo business—a premium service like its international passenger operation. It transports salmon from Chile, asparagus from Peru, fresh flowers from Ecuador, and other such perishables to the U.S. and Europe while flying high-value-to-weight merchandise such as computers, mobile phones, and small car parts from the U.S. and Europe to Latin America.

LAN is unusual among passenger carriers in its reliance on cargo revenue—accounting, by the second quarter of 2011, for 31% of its total revenue (compared with less than 5% for American, Delta, and United-Continental). Although Korean Air and Cathay Pacific both also derive about a third of their revenue from cargo, LAN is distinctive in that it transports fully 35% of its shipments in the belly of wide-body passenger aircraft, which serve most of its cargo destinations. In fact, the bulk of LAN's cargo business operates on the same route network with its passenger business.

In all three of LAN's models, the key to profitability is the same: flying more planes, more fully loaded, to more places. However, when LAN set out in 2007 to introduce no-frills flights on domestic routes, it knew it could not do that by combining passengers and cargo on those routes. The goal was to increase profitability and preempt the threat from some Latin American version of Ryanair or Southwest, initially on flights within Chile and Peru and later on routes to Argentina, Ecuador, and Colombia.

But on the one hand, demand for air-cargo transport was far lower in domestic markets than it was internationally, given that goods could instead be carried by truck, train, or boat. What's more, its local markets generated little demand for the perishables that LAN was transporting farther abroad. And perhaps most critically, the narrow-body aircraft used on the short-haul routes were not big enough to carry sufficient cargo.

On the other hand, passenger demand for LAN's domestic air travel is highly elastic: By lowering fares on short-haul routes by 20%, LAN could attract up to 40% more passengers, enabling it to invest in newer, more efficient planes, which could fly more hours per day. The implication was that the most direct (perhaps the only) way to increase capacity utilization for domestic flights was with low fares, made possible solely by offering a basic level of service to drive down costs.

This logic has been borne out, as lower fares have led to dramatic increases in demand: From 2006 to 2010, the number of passengers on LAN's domestic flights increased 83% within Chile, 123% in Peru, and 200% in Argentina, allowing LAN to reach its goal of increasing aircraft utilization on its short-haul routes from eight to 12 hours a day. LAN now holds the largest market share of passenger traffic within Chile and Peru and is increasing its market share in other South American countries.

LAN also has the largest market share of passenger traffic to and from Chile, Peru, and Ecuador, as well as approximately 37% of the Latin American air-cargo market, as its complementary full-service passenger and cargo operations have yielded many mutually reinforcing advantages. These include:

Maximal use of physical assets

Consider the following example: A LAN flight from Miami arrives in Santiago, Chile, at 5:00 AM. It continues to another Latin American city, say Bogotá, Lima, or Buenos Aires, to deliver cargo from the U.S. Then it returns to Santiago to fly customers back to Miami or New York, because passenger flights to the U.S. from South America are at night. Meanwhile, competitors with no cargo operation are forced to park their aircraft at Santiago's airport for most of the day. The advantages of increased utilization of as costly an asset as a wide-body aircraft are easy to see.

Reduction of the break-even load factor (BELF)

By combining cargo and passenger operations, LAN can profitably fly where other airlines cannot, because the number of passengers or amount of cargo it needs to break even on each flight is lower than if LAN were transporting only one or the other. In 2010, for instance, the BELF percentage for LAN's Santiago-Miami route would have been 68% if the aircraft had flown only passengers, but transporting cargo as well lowered it to 50%. What's more, without cargo, LAN's Santiago-Madrid-Frankfurt route, to take just one, would have terminated in Madrid, because going on to Frankfurt is not profitable when carrying only passengers.

Diversification of revenues and profits

By transporting both cargo and passengers, LAN can keep flying routes profitably when demand falls, as the two businesses seldom dip to the same degree in tandem. Even in the depths of the Great Recession in 2009, when cargo demand was down 10.1%, passenger travel dropped by only 3.5%. So LAN did not have to contract operations as much as its cargo-only competitors did, and it consequently was ready the next year to take advantage of renewed demand that those carriers could not accommodate.

Reduced threat of entry by other airlines

As LAN increases the number of routes it serves, it decreases the probability that other carriers can profitably enter into its markets.

One-stop shop for cargo in Latin America

The ability to fly more routes profitably creates a virtuous circle. More routes mean more value for customers, enabling LAN to charge premium prices, thereby generating revenue to support even more routes and to eventually become the one-stop shop for cargo distribution in Latin America. (See the exhibit "How two business models complement each other.") The rock group The Police, for instance, used LAN to transport a stage show that filled two jumbo jets for an eight-concert Latin American tour. Less exotic clients, such as smartphone and computer hardware makers, have proven similarly willing to pay a premium for the convenience of having a single company handle all their shipping needs in Latin America.

The Challenge of Managing Multiple Models

Why doesn't every airline do what LAN does? Part of the answer is historical: The Cueto family, one of the two groups that purchased LAN when the Chilean government fully privatized it, in 1994, had begun in the cargo business with Fast Air during the 1970s. So the family knew the business well and could readily see, in the context of a combined cargo and passenger service, the profit potential of LAN's international routes, its wide-body aircraft, and its reputation for reliability.

But to recognize the potential and to capitalize on it are two different things. To say that two models complement each other is not to say that combining them is easy. In fact, the learning curve

How two business models complement each other

Simultaneous investment in LAN Airlines' passenger and cargo businesses creates a virtuous circle by increasing volume and aircraft utilization, which decreases the break-even load factor and increases the attractiveness of new routes. Adding more routes leads to greater economies of scale and scope, boosts customers' willingness to pay, and increases revenues and profits— thereby providing a funding source for further expansion.

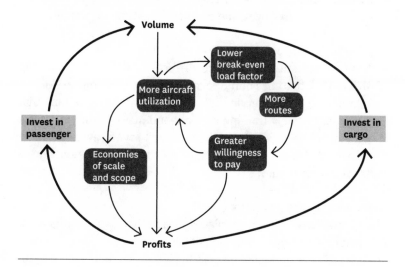

can be steep, favoring those, like LAN, that climb it first. Among LAN's chief challenges in combining its cargo and international passenger models, while keeping its low-cost model separate, were these:

Additional complexity

To plan for both businesses, LAN must dynamically coordinate a sophisticated passenger-yield management system, which raises and lowers ticket prices to manage demand levels, with an active cargo-capacity management system that similarly varies rates on cargo. LAN also needs to assign that cargo optimally to either the passenger or the freight planes, which it does through a complex logistics system that coordinates cargo and passengers. Given that both divisions are profit centers, possible conflicts must be managed carefully. Therefore, LAN has imposed an additional criterion for passenger fares that its global long-haul competitors do not need: The lowest passenger fare must be at least as large as the revenue that LAN would obtain if the weight burden of the passengers were allocated to cargo. In this way, LAN gives priority to carrying people in its wide-body passenger aircraft but also ensures that the minimum passenger fare covers the cost of cargo of similar weight.

Broader organizational skills

LAN's three businesses require different sales and marketing efforts and a sometimes mind-boggling variety of technical skills to maintain its premium services. For instance, at the same time that LAN was extensively training its flight and maintenance crews for its passenger business (ultimately winning it several awards for service), it needed to train employees in how to care for pigs and horses in its cargo-only planes.

Greater employee flexibility

Flying more planes to more places means that LAN's pilots must fly even on two hours' notice, half the time typical for a U.S. legacy airline. That would not be possible if LAN had not created a culture that fosters flexibility by instituting a performance-related pay and bonus structure, both for management and for administrative and flight personnel. Notably, though, in 2010 LAN's wages were a lower percentage of its total costs relative to the percentage at many U.S. and European carriers.

Additional investments

No two business models share all resources, of course. In Miami, for example, where LAN's cargo operations are headquartered, the company has almost 500,000 square feet of dedicated warehouse space and other cargo facilities that its passenger competitors do not need. Furthermore, to serve Latin America comprehensively, regulatory constraints preventing non-national companies from operating within certain countries have impelled LAN to create a series of separate companies for its no-frills short-haul passenger service: LAN Peru, LAN Ecuador, LAN Colombia, and LAN Argentina. It has also set up additional operating structures through alliances in Mexico and several other countries.

Distinguishing Complements from Substitutes

Operating three business models is clearly not without its risks—but meeting the challenge offers uniquely sustainable benefits. LAN was able to minimize the risks and capture the benefits by combining two complementary models and carefully keeping a competing model separate. But how did it tell which was which?

Our analysis suggests that to determine whether two business models are complements or substitutes, executives should consider two questions:

- To what extent do the business models share major physical assets?

- To what extent are the resources and capabilities that result from operating each business model compatible?

The greater the number of critical assets the models share, and the greater the number of shared capabilities and resources that result from the operation of the models, the more likely that combining the two models will yield a more valuable result. (See the exhibit "Are your business models complements or substitutes?")

In LAN's case, the major physical assets are its wide-body planes, which the cargo and international passenger models share but the low-cost domestic operations do not. Equally critical is the cascade of advantage-enhancing resources and capabilities produced by combining the cargo and full-fare passenger models:

- Decreasing the break-even load factor by combining cargo and passengers, thereby allowing LAN to fly to more places, creates value in both businesses and, thus, expands LAN's markets and revenues.

Are your business models complements or substitutes?

Business models are more likely to be complements rather than substitutes— and to generate greater value together than apart—if, when you consider these two questions, your answers fall closer to the right side of the spectrum than to the left.

	Question 1 To what extent do the business models share major physical assets?	
Substitute		**Complement**
Lesser		**Greater**
	Question 2 To what extent are the resources and capabilities that result from operating each business model compatible?	

- Using the growing revenues provided by cargo operations to underwrite better service to passengers and vice versa further increases customers' willingness to pay for both offerings.

- Flying to more places makes it harder for other airlines to enter and grow in the Latin American market for *either* cargo *or* passengers, which sustains LAN's advantage.

- The skills that LAN has had to develop to optimize the use of aircraft and the network of routes for both passengers and cargo have further increased barriers to imitation in both markets.

- LAN has become the leading passenger airline connecting Latin America to the rest of the world and *the* one-stop shop for cargo in the region. That increases switching costs for cargo customers and convenience for passengers, further boosting demand for both passenger and cargo service and thereby strengthening LAN's advantage.

LAN's low-cost domestic business does share in some of those capabilities and resources—the skills developed to efficiently schedule flights and maintain aircraft, the flexibility of its work-force, its understanding of the regulatory requirements for its various Latin American operations, and its capacity to fly customers and cargo to, from, and within Latin America. But LAN's critical physical assets can't be shared, and most of the capabilities and resources essential to the domestic operation—the brand, the reputation for low fares, the emphasis on efficiencies to lower costs—conflict with those of a premium, higher-cost offering. Those realities dictate that LAN operate the no-frills model separately.

It's far rarer for two business models to have *critical* assets, capabilities, and resources in common than not. That fact no doubt contributes both to the high failure rate of companies that use more than one model at a time and to the sense that firms that even contemplate running multiple models do so at their own risk.

But the lesson of LAN Airlines points to another form of risk—for LAN's competitors. By mastering three models—and by deeply understanding how complementary models generate unique opportunities—LAN has built, in both passenger and cargo service, formidable competitive advantages that are becoming increasingly difficult for competitors to overcome.

LAN's competitive advantage in international passenger service would vanish if the company did not have a thriving cargo business; likewise, its advantages in cargo would not exist without a blooming passenger business. Competitive strategy is all about building advantage by protecting a unique position and exploiting a distinctive set of resources and capabilities. Viewed in this light, the implementation of multiple business models is not a risk but rather a new tool for strategists. Properly applied, it will help firms boost their ability to create and capture value—and to gain durable advantage.

Originally published in January–February 2012. Reprint R1201M

Reaching the Rich World's Poorest Consumers

by Muhammad Yunus, Frédéric Dalsace,
David Menascé, and Bénédicte Faivre-Tavignot

POVERTY IS NOT JUST AN emerging-market problem. In the United States more than 45 million people, or 15% of the population, are officially poor, according to the Census Bureau. What's more, this percentage has increased every year but one (2006) since the 21st century began. At 16%, Japan is doing no better. And in the European Union almost 120 million people—one in every four—are classified as at risk of poverty or social exclusion.

In the past, businesses in the developed world have largely ignored the needs of these groups. To be sure, they know that not all their customers are rich, and many companies have invested significantly in creating low-cost products and services specifically tailored to people on a tight budget. Most automakers have offered low-budget cars for decades: The Model T Ford, the VW Beetle, the Mini Cooper, and the Citroën 2CV were in their time designed for what their manufacturers saw as the budget market. Low-cost "hard discounters" such as Aldi and Lidl in Europe and Market Basket in the United States have emerged relatively recently in the retail industry.

But the low-cost, low-price products and services that have traditionally served poorer consumers in Europe are usually still out of reach for the 25% who are at risk of poverty. Consumers in this group often can't buy essential products and services without significant aid from the state—whose ability to provide such aid is diminishing even as the need for it grows. Limited public transportation, for example, means that many poor people in rural districts must rely on aging, extremely cheap vehicles. Someone whose car breaks down may be out of work as a result.

In recent years a number of large corporations have started approaching problems of this kind in a new way. In 2009 Martin Hirsch, the former French high commissioner in charge of poverty alleviation, and Emmanuel Faber, then the food giant Danone's deputy general manager (now its CEO), came together to form the Action Tank—a not-for-profit association directed by Jacques Berger, of HEC. Through the Action Tank a number of leading multinationals have joined forces with NGOs and government organizations to experiment with developing social businesses in France.

"Social business" is a concept originally developed in the context of poor countries. Such a business has three key characteristics: First, it seeks to alleviate social problems, including all forms of poverty. Second, it must be run sustainably—that is, it should not lose money. Third, profits—when they exist—are reinvested in the business rather than funneled back to shareholders. Investors eventually get back only the money they initially invested. Danone and a growing number of other multinationals have for some time been engaged in social businesses in Bangladesh and other poor countries, but applications in the developed world are rare.

Among the first companies to join Danone in the Action Tank were the eye-care company Essilor, the construction giant Bouygues, the telecommunications group SFR, and the carmaker Renault. Early results from these companies' experiments suggest that the social business model is both an efficient way of fighting poverty and a productive source of new business ideas. Their ventures are sustainably

Idea in Brief

The Problem

Poverty reaches far beyond emerging markets. In the European Union alone, almost 120 million people—nearly 25% of the population—are deemed at risk of poverty or social exclusion.

The Current Approach

Corporations usually try to meet the needs of poorer consumers with low-cost, low-price offers while still making a profit. They have improved access to many products and services, but a substantial number of consumers are still largely excluded.

The Solution

In France, the not-for-profit Action Tank is experimenting with an alternative: the social business model. It differs in a number of ways from traditional low-cost models—beginning with the fact that its primary goal is to solve social problems for customers.

providing high-quality products and services to very poor people at rock-bottom prices.

Essilor's social business, Optique Solidaire, is a good example. Working with all the company's supply chain partners, including insurance companies, it has succeeded in driving down the cost of a pair of high-quality reading glasses to poor pensioners from 230–300 euros to less than 30 euros. After spending 15 months working out the offering and three months conducting an experiment in Marseille, Optique Solidaire has built a network of more than 500 "solidarity retailers" across France. They are opticians who have volunteered to spend some of their time selling the glasses at a sharply reduced profit margin. Target customers—people over 60 with minimal resources—receive a voucher and a letter from their insurance company telling them about the offer and supplying the address of the closest participating optician. Essilor's goal is to recruit 1,000 retailers in France and to equip 250,000 to 300,000 people with glasses they could not otherwise afford.

In the following pages we present the social business model that is emerging from experiments like this and demonstrate how radically it differs from traditional low-cost business models. The new model, perhaps counterintuitively, looks more like that of a high-end solutions provider than that of a discount supplier. Obviously, financial profit is not its goal. We will describe the business benefits, both tangible and intangible, that social businesses can provide and the factors that contribute most to their success.

The Model

Let's begin by looking at the value propositions that social business models offer. These typically involve:

Customer exclusivity

Unlike low-cost models, social business models are exclusive: Companies determine up front which and how many consumers the program will serve, and no one else is eligible for the offer. The target may be broad. For instance, SFR and the French charity Emmaüs, which focuses on the homeless, regard all poor people who have a mobile phone as eligible for the services offered through their project Téléphonie Solidaire. But the target may also be narrow, such as poor consumers older than 60 (Essilor), poor families with a child aged six months to 24 months (Danone), or poor consumers who need a car to get—or keep—a job (Renault).

In determining eligibility, social businesses usually work with nonprofits, which rely in turn on local associations and public programs to find potential beneficiaries. This approach also reduces companies' costs.

High-quality products and services

In a low-cost business model, every consumer, whether poor or not, evaluates the trade-off between the company's standard and low-cost offers. If they are too similar, the company runs the risk of cannibalizing its standard offer. Thus it must downgrade key attributes in the cheaper offer to create a distinct trade-off.

In a social business model, the offer can remain unchanged if the economics allow. This is important, because the goal of the social business is precisely to give poor people access to an *existing* product or service whenever possible. Danone, Renault, and SFR provide poor customers with products and services identical to those offered to richer ones. The only difference in Optique Solidaire's offering is a limited assortment of frames; lens quality remains the same.

The commitment to high quality means that social businesses don't lower their costs by redesigning products or manufacturing processes, as low-cost businesses may do. They focus on changing the economics of sales and distribution. The solution is often to partner with nonprofits or to work with distributors on a noncommercial basis, as Essilor did. And as we'll see, companies that devise an integrated, solution-style offering can offset costs in one component with savings in other components.

Carefully designed solutions

Unlike low-cost companies, which are defined largely in terms of products and services, a social business often (though not always) expresses its value proposition as a solution to a social problem customers have. Renault's Mobiliz is a case in point. The project's goal is to resolve transportation issues for poor people. In cities, Mobiliz works with the NGO Wimoov to find the cheapest form of mobility for working poor people, whether it be the metro, buses, or bicycles. In rural areas, however, the project's customers need access to a cheap car and affordable maintenance, which Mobiliz provides through a network of "solidarity garages." Network participants (garages owned or franchised by Renault) dedicate a portion of their time and resources to repairing damaged or broken cars for qualifying customers at a nominal cost. The French NGOs Wimoov, FASTT, and UDAF are responsible for "recruiting" customers.

An often-important part of social business solutions is promoting behavior change on the part of customers. Danone's Projet Malin, a joint program with the French Red Cross, provides low-income parents with affordable and nutritious food for children, educational materials, and courses delivered by independent third parties. "The purpose of our program is to ensure that children are well nourished," says Benjamin Cavalli, of the Red Cross. "We ask the mothers if they want to attend an educational workshop to develop good nutritional practices. Many do." (Programs must take care not to seem patronizing; for example, there's no need to lecture poor commuters on how to travel.)

Thinking in terms of solutions can help companies with the challenge of costs. Since 2000, French law has required that a city of more than 3,500 inhabitants that is part of an "urban center" of more than 50,000 must have at least 25% of its dwellings qualify as social (public) housing. Understandably, companies doing this kind of construction try to minimize direct costs through efficiency. But Bouygues realized that building apartments inexpensively didn't necessarily make them affordable over the long term.

Working with the Action Tank, the company estimated that in the Paris area, construction accounts for less than 30% of total housing costs over the life of a building. Land accounts for about 12%, financing for 15%, maintenance and repair for 12%, and usage (heat, electricity, water, garbage collection, and other running expenses) for about 35%. So the company has broadened its scope to offer a more integrated service. It has proposed innovations such as decreasing the size of individual units in order to build in neighborhoods with better connections to public transportation (an idea borrowed from the hotel industry), creating a common laundry room (unusual in France), asking tenants to take care of the cleaning (including the garbage), and setting up efficient water distribution systems. Some of these innovations would entail up-front costs, but the downstream savings would more than cover them.

The Hidden Payoffs

The primary purpose of a low-cost business is to create shareholder value by generating profits. Although the business makes products accessible to poor consumers, that is merely a means of delivering on its promise to shareholders. Because a social business seeks to alleviate social problems sustainably, however, its profits are plowed back into the company. But that's not to say that social businesses yield only social returns. In fact, the spillover effects of creating them may in the long run be as commercially valuable as the profits of a low-cost business. Those effects include uncovering opportunities for innovation in new markets, motivating employees, and enhancing the company's reputation—along with demand for its products and services.

Breakthrough innovation

Social businesses have long been recognized as what Rosabeth Moss Kanter, of Harvard Business School, has called "beta sites for innovation." Emmanuel Faber has described Danone's social business in Bangladesh, which started in 2005, as "the best R&D lab ever." To be sure, low-cost businesses do often trigger innovation in processes and design, but the innovation of social businesses tends to be more radical, because they are trying to maintain the original quality of their products and services. As we saw with Bouygues, this forces them to break away from product-centered innovation and focus instead on *consumer-centered* innovation.

François Rouvier, the manager of Mobiliz, says, "Developing the Dacia [Renault's low-cost car in Europe] was a formidable challenge for Renault. We started with existing cars and left no stone unturned to make it cheaper. In a sense, we were going downward. But in the social business model we put the constrained customer, not the product, at the center of the action, and we seek to help her go upward. This is a whole new mindset."

As a result, companies can identify ways to increase access to their commercial products as well. For example, Renault's consumer-centered research revealed that the prohibitive cost of qualifying for a driver's license was a major reason that fewer and fewer young people in France were buying cars. The company teamed up with ECF, France's leading driving school, to develop a computer game for learners. By speeding up the learning process, it can drastically cut the overall cost of lessons.

Social business models also spark innovation through the high level of collaboration they involve. In particular, they enable companies to leverage existing capabilities in the not-for-profit sector. Essilor has launched several commercial projects as a result of its experiment. In Southeast Asia, for example, it has applied the idea of sending vouchers to customers via a third party. Rather than waiting for people to visit opticians and buy glasses from them, Essilor works with corporations that send letters to their employees offering to share or even bear the cost of glasses. This improves both employees' quality of life and the quality of their work—a triple win that benefits Essilor, its customers, and their employers.

Motivation

Our experience shows that social business models generate a lot of motivation and meaning for workers, who are often less engaged when their employer's sole purpose is to make shareholders happy. One of Renault's goals for Mobiliz was to strengthen the social DNA of the company; the name stands for both the mobility of the consumers Renault serves and the mobilization of its people. The company has been surprised by how positively its dealer network and sales force have reacted.

"We thought Mobiliz would not be welcome, because by definition the model makes it impossible to make money," says Claire Martin, Renault's vice president for corporate social responsibility. "But we received encouragement from people throughout the firm. The reaction of the sales department was so favorable that we are now facing a highly unexpected problem: too many garages that volunteer and not enough low-income car owners who can be identified and channeled through our partnering NGOs." This level of enthusiasm almost certainly translates into higher rates of employee retention and productivity.

Reputation

Large corporations that introduce low-cost products are quickly suspected of trying to make money on the backs of the poor, which can damage their overall brand image. For instance, after Danone introduced low-cost yogurts on the French market in 2010, public reaction forced the company to discontinue the product line. Nutriset, the world leader in emergency food for developing countries, had to abandon two consecutive attempts to sell nutrition bars to very low income consumers in France, because social activists argued that it

How social businesses differ from low-cost businesses

Here's a quick comparison of the two models:

	Low-cost	Social
VALUE PROPOSITION	**Objective** To make a profit by improving access to products and services	To improve access to essential products and services in a financially sustainable manner
	Exclusivity Any consumer can buy the offer	The company decides who the targets are and how to filter them
	Quality Lower, to avoid cannibalizing the regular offer	Unchanged
	Focus Low-price products and services	Affordable solutions to social problems
SOURCE OF VALUE	**Operations** Reconfiguring the production supply chain to reduce costs	Reconfiguring the distribution supply chain to reach targeted consumers
	Partnerships Optional co-creation with profit-maximizing organizations	Required co-creation with third parties that have a social welfare objective
	Innovation Product-centered	Customer-centered and ecosystemic
	Employee motivation Weak	Strong
	Reputation May be quite low	Likely to be high

was an immoral way to make money and that the goal should be to offer "real meals."

But when a company starts a social business, which is expressly not for profit, it can change stakeholders' perceptions. The model breaks down barriers and helps the company build new relationships based on trust. Emmanuelle Vignaud, Danone's brand marketing manager, says, "Social business projects show that our firm has a more comprehensive and long-term mindset. We are not considered 'predators' anymore, which has concrete consequences. One key pediatrician, who had refused to meet with us before, agreed to be interviewed for more than two hours to help us understand how baby food will evolve. We have also earned the trust of two pediatricians' union leaders, who are involved on the board of Projet Malin. These relationships could be immensely useful as we look for new product ideas going forward."

To be sure, the low-cost model has a long history—probably best exemplified by the Model T Ford—of providing people with access to goods and services. Its ability to generate financial returns aligns it with the goals of most companies. We believe, however, that the social business model has the potential to provide even greater access, and its spillover benefits can create value over the long term, making it a significant alternative to low-cost business ventures.

Making the Model Work

Veolia, Total, La Poste, and Michelin are among the large organizations that are now joining the Action Tank to experiment with social businesses. The success of such projects in France has spurred the creation of action tanks in Portugal and Belgium to help companies develop similar programs. Our experience in France has enabled us to pinpoint the crucial factors.

Always put the social goal first

Companies must keep in mind the point we made earlier: Social businesses have *social goals* and *business spillovers,* not the reverse. If a social business is created to stimulate innovation or improve reputation, it will generate suspicion among its partners, threaten the cooperation needed for innovation, and look like corporate hypocrisy to company employees. This doesn't mean, of course, that you can't talk about the spillover effects—just that they have to take second place or you won't get them at all.

Be patient and selective in partnering

It takes time to construct the right model for the social problem you are addressing. (Schneider Electric has worked with the Action Tank since the latter's inception, but because it's primarily a B2B firm, selecting a project was challenging. Schneider is only now starting to experiment with measuring energy consumption for poor people.) Negotiations are necessary both internally and with external ecosystem partners. Finding the right organizations to partner with is difficult: You need to understand their cultures and mindsets—especially when they're non-profits, whose participation and credibility are essential for success. The Action Tank has been helpful in making connections and deepening understanding of partnership challenges, and many of the world's top consultancies have practices that specialize in social ventures.

Keep it as simple as you can

Poor people in developed countries often have a lot of choice. SFR and Emmaüs have identified more than 300 social service programs in France. But each has its own, sometimes complicated, processes and eligibility criteria, and poor people with limited time find it hard to make an informed choice among them. Even when a social business can identify all potential beneficiaries (as Optique Solidaire was able to), it's generally able to reach only about 30% of them. Some social businesses are now developing traditional push marketing initiatives such as advertising and couponing to raise public awareness of their products and services.

Start local

Don't try to launch a national program from scratch. Figuring out how to collaborate with nonprofits is better handled on a small scale. Luckily, the customer exclusivity of social businesses makes it easy to run experiments. Essilor needed 18 months to work out the right model including its pilot project in Marseille, and Danone's Projet Malin is still being refined in just four cities. Determining how to filter customers can be especially challenging.

Social business is still in its infancy. Early evidence suggests, however, that it can help companies looking for market-based solutions to poverty issues. Its business spillovers—innovation, motivation, and reputation—are significant. More important, it is demonstrating that large corporations can be powerful agents of social change when they partner with other organizations. And social businesses can unify all society's organizations, including businesses, nonprofits, and government agencies. That is no small achievement, because we need all our talents in the fight against poverty.

Originally published in March 2015. Reprint R1503B

About the Contributors

ELIZABETH J. ALTMAN is an assistant professor of strategic management at the Manning School of Business at the University of Massachusetts Lowell and a visiting scholar at Harvard Business School. She was formerly a vice president of strategy and business development at Motorola. Follow her on Twitter @lizaltman.

STEVE BLANK is a consulting associate professor at Stanford University and a lecturer and National Science Foundation principal investigator at the University of California at Berkeley and Columbia University. He has participated in eight high-tech start-ups as either a cofounder or an early employee.

DAVID J. BRYCE is an associate professor of strategy at Brigham Young University's Marriott School of Management and adjunct associate professor of management at The Wharton School, University of Pennsylvania.

RAMON CASADESUS-MASANELL is a professor at Harvard Business School.

SANGEET PAUL CHOUDARY is the founder and CEO of Platform Thinking Labs and an entrepreneur-in-residence at INSEAD. He is the author (with Marshall W. Van Alstyne and Geoffrey G. Parker) of *Platform Revolution* (W.W. Norton & Company, 2016).

CLAYTON M. CHRISTENSEN is the Kim B. Clark Professor of Business Administration at Harvard Business School.

SARAH CLIFFE is Editorial Director at *Harvard Business Review*.

FRÉDÉRIC DALSACE is an associate professor of marketing and holds the Social Business, Enterprise and Poverty chair at HEC Paris.

JEFFREY H. DYER is the Horace Beesley Professor of Strategy at Brigham Young University's Marriott School.

BÉNÉDICTE FAIVRE-TAVIGNOT is an affiliate professor at HEC Paris and the academic director of its master's program in sustainable development.

KARAN GIROTRA is a professor at INSEAD in Fontainebleau, France, and a coauthor, with Serguei Netessine, of *The Risk-Driven Business Model: Four Questions That Will Define Your Company* (HBR Press, 2014). Follow him on Twitter @Girotrak.

ANDREI HAGIU is a visiting associate professor of technological innovation, entrepreneurship, and strategic management at the MIT Sloan School of Management. Follow him on Twitter @theplatformguy.

NILE W. HATCH is an associate professor of entrepreneurship at Brigham Young University's Marriott School of Management.

MARK W. JOHNSON is cofounder and senior partner of the strategy consulting firm Innosight and author of *Reinvent Your Business Model: Seizing the White Space for Transformative Growth* (HBR Press, 2018).

HENNING KAGERMANN is a former CEO of SAP.

STELIOS KAVADIAS is the Margaret Thatcher Professor of Enterprise Studies in Innovation and Growth at the University of Cambridge's Judge Business School and the director of its Entrepreneurship Centre.

KOSTAS LADAS is an associate at the Entrepreneurship Centre at Cambridge Judge Business School.

CHRISTOPH LOCH is a professor at and the director (dean) of the University of Cambridge's Judge Business School.

JOAN MAGRETTA is a senior associate at the Institute for Strategy and Competitiveness at Harvard Business School. She is the author of *Understanding Michael Porter: The Essential Guide to Competition and Strategy* (HBR Press, 2011).

RITA GUNTHER McGRATH is a professor of management at Columbia Business School and a globally recognized expert on strategy, innovation, and growth with an emphasis on corporate entrepreneurship.

DAVID MENASCÉ is the managing director of Azao, a consulting company specializing in social business, and an affiliate professor at HEC Paris.

SERGUEI NETESSINE is the vice dean for global initiatives and the Dhirubhai Ambani Professor of Innovation and Entrepreneurship at the University of Pennsylvania's Wharton School and a coauthor, with Karan Girotra, of *The Risk-Driven Business Model: Four Questions That Will Define Your Company* (HBR Press, 2014). Follow him on Twitter @snetesin.

GEOFFREY G. PARKER is a professor of engineering at Dartmouth College and is a fellow at the MIT Center for Digital Business. He is the author (with Marshall W. Van Alstyne and Sangeet Paul Choudary) of *Platform Revolution* (W.W. Norton & Company, 2016).

JORGE TARZIJÁN is a professor in the School of Management at the Pontificia Universidad Católica de Chile, in Santiago.

MARSHALL W. VAN ALSTYNE is a professor and chair of the information systems department at Boston University and a fellow at the MIT Initiative on the Digital Economy. He is the author (with Geoffrey G. Parker and Sangeet Paul Choudary) of *Platform Revolution* (W.W. Norton & Company, 2016).

MUHAMMAD YUNUS, the founder of Grameen Bank, a microfinance business that first operated in rural Bangladesh, won the 2006 Nobel Peace Prize.

Index

The most important management ideas all in one place.

We hope you enjoyed this book from *Harvard Business Review*. Now you can get even more with HBR's 10 Must Reads Boxed Set. From books on leadership and strategy to managing yourself and others, this 6-book collection delivers articles on the most essential business topics to help you succeed.

HBR's 10 Must Reads Series

The definitive collection of ideas and best practices on our most sought-after topics from the best minds in business.

- Change Management
- Collaboration
- Communication
- Emotional Intelligence
- Innovation
- Leadership
- Making Smart Decisions

- Managing Across Cultures
- Managing People
- Managing Yourself
- Strategic Marketing
- Strategy
- Teams
- The Essentials

hbr.org/mustreads

Buy for your team, clients, or event.
Visit hbr.org/bulksales for quantity discount rates.